Skip Tracer

Skip Tracer

Jive Poetic

Liveright Publishing Corporation
A Division of W. W. Norton & Company
Independent Publishers Since 1923

For information about permission to reproduce selections from this book,
write to Permissions, Liveright Publishing Corporation, a division of
W. W. Norton & Company, Inc., 500 Fifth Avenue, New York, NY 10110

For information about special discounts for bulk purchases, please contact
W. W. Norton Special Sales at specialsales@wwnorton.com or 800-233-4830

Manufacturing by Versa Press
Book design by Chris Welch
Production manager: Lauren Abbate

ISBN 978-1-324-09316-9

Liveright Publishing Corporation, 500 Fifth Avenue, New York, N.Y. 10110
www.wwnorton.com

W. W. Norton & Company Ltd., 15 Carlisle Street, London W1D 3BS

1 2 3 4 5 6 7 8 9 0

Contents

Cassette Single

Reels

Crossfader

Turntables

Records

Maxi Single

Instrumentals

Livestream

Bonus Track

Skip Tracer

Introduction

I've never lived in a house without records. My mother and uncles had extensive album collections. They started plugging in these gray and black headphones so I could listen to their LPs when I was seven years old. The music, cover art, and liner notes kept me occupied for as long as the songs played. I pretended the tracks told the story that unfolded on the jackets, and it was my job to dream up the unpictured scenes; this continued until it was time to flip the record over. I'm not sure how anybody else was raised, but kids weren't allowed to touch record players where I'm from. My mother kept hers in the living room with the good furniture; there was no plastic on the couches, but they were white, and you know what that meant. Actually, to be clear, it was the front room. Our apartment had two living rooms. The one all the way in front was for adults. The other was for everybody, but mostly kids and video games. Being in the front room, or upfront as we called it, made me feel grown but not enough to touch that turntable.

My mother and uncles were worried about me dropping the needle improperly and damaging the grooves. Some records were limited releases, printed on colored vinyl, or contained bonus tracks. All of them would become rare, valuable, and, in some cases, irreplaceable. They never had to remind me of the rules. It was simple: sit still, listen, and there won't be any trouble.

My mother played two records for me all of the time. *Off the Wall* by Michael Jackson told me it was time to wake up for school. I never got tired of it. The cover felt perfectly in sync with the title. It featured Michael Jackson standing slightly away from an exposed brick background, but that wasn't the off-the-wall part. He wore a black tuxedo with white socks. There was no way anybody in my house would've allowed me to dress like that. My stepfather wore suits every day, even if he was going to the corner store. He had rules about clothes: don't pair belts with suspenders, and pants should not be lighter than your shirt. Michael Jackson didn't care about dress codes, not even the sometimes-always-never rule for buttons on sports coats and blazers. His jacket was completely unbuttoned because he was the king of pop and could do whatever he wanted. He glided backward when he danced, wore a sequined glove, had a pet chimpanzee, and his shoes made the sidewalk light up when he walked. Bright. Glowing. Black suit. White socks. Michael Jackson. Off the wall.

The second album was *Too Hot to Handle* by Heatwave. Track two, "Boogie Nights," told me when it was time for bed. The opening harp strings sounded like the beginning of a dreamscape—they drew me into the illustrated album cover (into a scene so hot, everything [even the fire hydrant] was melting). I usually made it a few bars into the vocals before falling asleep on the carpet. I remembered putting on the headphones and hearing the music but never how I got in bed. The members of Heatwave probably wouldn't describe their music as funk-lullaby, but that's how it worked on me, and that's why it's still one of my favorite records.

I copped *Long Live the Kane* by Big Daddy Kane on cassette when I was old enough to purchase music. One of the singles, "Ain't No Half Steppin," borrowed its hook and title from a song by the same name on that Heatwave album I had heard so many times before. The woven samples reminded me of African American quilting traditions. Recognizing the base materials for this song made my ears sensitive to the sonic fabric of hip-hop music in a new way. I grew curious about how cutting and spinning old tracks into new ones was possible. My classmates became obsessed with sports, athletes, and stats while I focused on albums like

By All Means Necessary by Boogie Down Productions (BDP), *Paid in Full* by Eric B. and Rakim, *3 Feet High and Rising* by De La Soul, *Strictly Business* by EPMD, and *It Takes a Nation of Millions to Hold Us Back* by Public Enemy. I recorded rap shows off the radio and television, transcribed lyrics, and memorized songs.

A friend loaned me a mixtape in high school. It stayed in my Walkman until the tape popped from rewinding without pushing the stop button first. The DJ, Rap Master Shane, scratched, gave shoutouts, made remixes, and dropped songs radio stations didn't even have. I imagined myself being on tape like this one day. Like a guitarist imitating chord progressions on an invisible guitar, my hands would play air DJ whenever I heard a DJ scratching. In college, after I'd saved enough money, I ordered my first set of turntables from an advertisement in the back of *The Source* magazine and started shopping for vinyl records. I already had *Lyte as a Rock* by MC Lyte and "Tramp" by Salt-N-Pepa, but I needed more. The square plastic bags from record stores could have fit in my backpack, but I always carried them in my hand and hoped people would ask me if I was a DJ on my way home. I've accumulated a couple thousand twelve-inch singles and full-length LPs between then and now. They all have backstories that come to mind when I pull them from the shelves.

I'm a DJ now and have been for decades. My favorite part of being behind the turntables is making people sing along to the records. Watching them dance feels good, but my adrenaline rushes when people are pushed beyond their footwork and into a trance where they shout lyrics with their eyes closed; it feels like being choirmaster and pastor at a church where the congregation catches the spirit from the right selection. As powerful as these moments are, this joyful frenzy is also as delicate as the vinyl is fragile. Pops, scratches, and skips in the grooves interfere with the energy exchange. They split my attention between the dance floor and the spinning records while I dig through my crates for an emergency replacement song. Crackling sounds that continue for too long leave the crowd half dancing and half waiting for a skip to trip up the momentum and kill the vibe.

One of my grandfather's nicknames was Skip. Everyone who knew him told me how he could change the mood of a room. His sisters spoke about how handsome and charming he was. My uncles remember being so scared of him that their noses would bleed if he looked at them too hard. Imagine being so terrified of a person that your stress response was a bloody nose. Unfortunately, he passed away before my mind could collect and save anything more than the island in his voice and time lines creased into his face. His life gets told back to me through pictures and memories. Like music on vinyl, some records were given to me fully intact and still play smoothly. Others are scratched snippets that get looped and replayed. Through poems and prose, I archived some that I remember, dug up buried ones, and tried to repair others that pop and skip.

The elders in my family didn't tell us much about our family's journey to the United States. When I was a child listening to records in the front room, this need for secrecy was confusing. My friends had huge families and stories about being from down south. I wanted to talk about my family too, but the older generation kept the stories from us. My grandparents' silence about our history makes more sense to me now as an adult living in a time of mass deportation and widespread criminalization of immigrants. My grandparents were here during World War II and saw Japanese Americans placed in internment camps due to fears of espionage. My mother and uncles grew up during the Cuban Missile Crisis. I was in middle school when the United States invaded Panama. We had family living in both countries. Giving us too many records at one time could have made the government find us suspicious.

My grandmother kept most of our family records in a large Bible. She recorded births and deaths and saved pictures with names and places written on the backs. The entries and images date back to the 1800s. What's left of them, including the Bible, sits in my bedroom. This inheritance makes me wonder about my lost family members, their forgotten voices, and their fading stories. Like playing two records simultaneously on my turntables, I often arrange pictures from different eras next to each other and try to draw connections between them. I've spent years researching these family records. Following clues in the archive has taken me from country to country to discover new stories and reconnect with previously unknown family members. I thought about how this book would look during the journey. The original idea was to present this project as a printed mixtape because it blends different records: printed, photographic, and oral. After composing the sections, I realized how it extended beyond the original metaphor and became an actual sound system. For some, this simply means stereo and speaker. In West Indian culture, a sound system includes selectas behind turntables, DJs on microphones, music collections, and equipment. Between these pages you will find live DJ sets, dubplates, multiple speakers, and tracks that play while others skip. Records still get mixed and recorded, but there are also points where text gets sampled and reused; some images serve as cover art for sections while others function as the source of reverbs, echoes, and interpolations that appear in the stanzas and paragraphs; time also gets rewound and fast-forwarded in this collection. Revisiting these experiences opens room for new observations, perspectives, and questions. These occurrences get pointed out before, during, and after they happen in the text. Using poems, prose, and images to manipulate time puts me face-to-face with past, present, and future versions of myself. When this happens in the text, I address everybody with second-person singular and plural pronouns. As *Skip Tracer* spins, there are beats when I am you and me, and we are all of us in the mix.

8-track
cassette

in my hand

        a couple

                backstories

                        from the shelves

Go Home

My neighborhood was hip-hop
and soul
and funk
and fistfight
and gun pull
and smoke clear
and finger cross for speaker-box-kick-drum to return
the block party
without missing a step. My mother used the explosions
to teach survival. Rule number one
always know when it is time to go home:
summer camp was free lunch in the park
then back home; trip to Manhattan then back home.
No matter where you were, if those streetlights came on
and you were not home
a problem.

    Don't make concern turn magnifying glass to find you.
    We still haven't solved what happened to Little Tasha.

And mamma used to say, police cars,
sirens, screams, cries, tears, all
emergency vehicles. Be aware of how far away they are,
how fast that far closed closer
how close that far was to/o late.
To them, we, always the most almost riot.
To us, they, always the most almost panic
because we have not forgotten
Carmella Stevenson would be alive
had paramedics not lost their grip
on urgency.

Mamma used to say, distraction will get you killed.
Pay attention to your environment.
Pay attention
to your environment; people are temperamental
environments; they change without warning.
Somebody said, *I'm going to kill Rasta Mike*;
                said,   *going to* and *kill*
in the same sentence; we didn't see Rasta Mike again
until a dark alley coughed up his body.

Never let your mouth write a check your ass can't cash

careful when cashing a check not written to your ass.
To be nosy is to be suicidal
on Jefferson Avenue. Exercise caution
around strange animals. Mamma used to say
language is a strange animal.
When tone & posture clash
teeth and claws will be inside jokes
between high-fives and knee-slaps.

when summer camp extended
beyond day trips and Styrofoam lunch trays
counselors spoke to me in street slang
and condescension. Their humor
taught my skin to feel Black in mixed company.

To feel Black in mixed company is to know
sidewinders slither sideways through subtext.
As soon as you recognize the hiss, do not run.
Do not cry. Thin skin will get you eaten alive
in these streets where we still do not know
what happened to Little Tasha,
still do not know who killed Rasta Mike,
still do not need to not know what happened to you too.
You have instincts for a reason; use them
like childhood streetlights. They will always tell you
when it is time to go home.

Stagedive

It's 6 PM. Water should be running. Plates should be clanking. Silverware should have dropped. The mother, in her bedroom, knows what it means when her son is too quiet. She hasn't heard any wineglasses break, but she continues reading her textbooks. She is a grad student studying psychology. Today will probably find its way into a paper she writes. The only music playing, a song in the boy's head. He tries to ignore it, but the drum loops his thoughts to the beat. A Kangol, Adidas, and a gold rope replace his glow-in-the-dark Go-Bot pajamas. He doesn't know his mother peeks in to see him bopping at the sink; because he is approximately where he was supposed to be, she quietly returns to her studies. Her last look didn't reveal how his good sense had already dried its hands, threw down the towel, and walked toward the front door. She usually catches this earlier, but today she is late to the party. The instrumentation in his mind is now being spit into his hand. This happens often enough for her not to look up when she tells him, *you can rap and beatbox after your work is done.* Unfortunately, the music is too loud. Her shoutouts are drowned-out background sounds. If there is such a thing as a hip-hop Holy Ghost, it has already turned him into a Biz Markie song; instead of washing dishes with his hands, he is making music with his mouth.

It's 6:15. A chair sliding across the floor startles the highlighter from the mother's hand. The boy, who went in with the good intention of doing his job, is now headlining at a rap concert where he has just fallen off of the stage during an unscripted dance number. His foot is hooked on the oven door handle because he tried to jump up and land in a handstand. She was right, this was no time for beatboxing. It was an even worse time for new b-boy moves, but he was standing on l-i-n-o-l-e-u-m, and in 1986, those letters together spell dance floor. He gathers his feet but can't collect his words. She doesn't say anything because she knows who her son is. A year ago, he tried to start a cat rehoming business with his friends and ended up in the hospital after being attacked by a pack of stray kittens they lured into the house. Nobody in the emergency room was surprised. They remembered the rusty nail jammed through his thumb after sword fighting with broomsticks he and the same friends found outside. His mother still hasn't said anything. She isn't even shaking her head. This will be one of the moments she points at when she says, *parenting doesn't come with instructions.* In the grand scheme of her son being who he is, today really isn't so bad. This week, he only fell in the kitchen because he thought he was a rap star. Last week, he hit his head on concrete because he thought he was a stunt car.

Inverse

The boy still looks down

new sneakers rebuild his body
into Knight Rider. His heart speeds
from the fuel injection. He kicks his feet
against the ground. The sound assures traction
before a five-foot drop. Onlooking church ladies
gasp, a group prayer for his life.

      He still rocks back and forth.

Nobody knows
this is not the universe where he lives:
not the church ladies
not the screaming mother
not the me life will make out of him.

      He still hits the gas.

In this timeline he never gets to
not buy puppies on his computer
never gets to not see his uncle before he dies
never gets to not forgive his father for mistakes
he never gets to grow to
understand.

He is still a running engine.

Where gravity is a DMV worker
daring anybody to get out of line
luck is a security guard
gambling second chances on lunch break.

He still takes off.

He never survives
a train under the World Trade Center
a landlord who buys arsonists wholesale
a pandemic that makes coffins out of the city.

He is still in midair.

Folded hands won't save him
in this space-time. Today is the day

he falls.

Home School

Mom slides Blue Magic
down my scalp. Three fingers
steady my forehead. Through the reflection
in the mirror she says noose
when she means necktie; she says, they will find loopholes
after they kill you; she says, they will hide behind badges
and blame everything except their uniforms:
point at bandanas and accuse crossfire;
point at sneakers and accuse robbery;
point at you and accuse accident,
blame death in custody on you
as if your will to live was an act of being your own rope
to the lynching. It doesn't matter how you dress
they will always see you the color of a crowbar
cracking a window; dark and terrifying
like a wallet mistaken for a gun. No cap,
no gown,
no diploma will save you. Mom finishes
to answer the smell from the stove; burning air
and Afro Sheen means my sister is next.
The grooming will be similar, but the comb
will be on fire.

Catholic School: Day 1

The transcript says,
student goes by middle name.

       ~~. . . first name,~~ a lot
handed down
vacant
and overrun
with rusted barstools
and quarter-cut straws
for the snowfall

The teacher reads none of this

between syllables
the remains of a mosque   in the wilted metal
she assumes. The crucifix
around her neck squirms
a reenactment
of the crusades. She settles on   splintered wood planking

what school calls his Christian name

        a path to a premonition

a memorial   where one drink
turns a bloodline into ruins

roped off with caution tape.

Catholic School: Week 3

The teacher and I are in a place
where we kind of understand each other:
she asks a question
then I ask a question
then she says, *principal's office*
then I ask another question
then she says, *parent-teacher conference.*
We both want today to be different
but there is a survey on her desk.
It has little dots from her pencil tapping
self-restraint; she is tired of me
and I am tired of her
multiple-choice obstacles
on paper; this one says   *Denomination*
Methodist as an option
by itself: ~~African~~ *Methodist* ~~Episcopal.~~

My silence, a waiting room
an offering of empty space for   a recognizable congregation:
                                          red, black, and green shield
                                          cross and anvil
                                          drummer in the corner
                                          usher in a white dress
this omission of Black church   pianos and choirs
a strike through   hymnals and Sunday schools
                                          and gospel plotting

          Underground Railroad tracks.

My hand never rises. She says,
*let's run through this questionnaire
one more time.* It's a reset steeplechase.
The bell rings. I don't move
again. She goes off.

Catholic School, Fourth Grade: Thanksgiving Break

Before they're old enough to want to know
if we think OJ did it
or why we voted for Obama
or why they can't say *the n word*
we learn they want us to answer
for everybody who looks like us   Black People
in fourth grade. They ask what we eat
for Thanksgiving. We give them everything
already on their tables: turkey
                    stuffing
                    and cranberry sauce   I'm unsure about sharing
                                           curry shrimp
                                           collard green
                                           macaroni and cheese
                                           or cornbread.
                                           I keep them separate
                                           with sweet potato pies
                                           and rice & peas

                    rolls and butter,
and everything sounds gravy.
We give forks and knives and trust them
with nothing they need to soak or boil
for days;   they get no sorrel
                                           no ackee
                                           no saltfish

their noses are still turned up
from when we explained
oxtail browning in our kitchen
like nobody's business.

Thanksgiving Dinner

Every year a different woman was designated to make the rice & peas for our family's holiday dinner. The honor was handed to my mother for the first time this year. My grandfather, at the head of the table, looked at his sister to cue my mother into the dining room. The plan was for her to step through the doorway as the last syllable of her name exited into the air. At this pace, she would end up next to my grandfather as Aunt Mary's introduction finished. The only thing that might have been missing from this orchestration was background music to softly float my mother into the room, but what melody could be more appropriate than our anticipation. We were the harmony our mood needed until my mother uncovered the dish: the rice was white, the peas were intact, and the whole family took note.

The comments were piano hammers hitting my mother's chords. The first came from the middle of the table: *Well, if we were back home, she would have soaked the peas overnight;* that sharp was followed by a flat: *. . . back home, she wouldn't have rinsed the peas after she boiled them.* Nobody, not even her father, defended her; this traumatic intermission continued until a spare pot of rice & peas was ushered into the room; like a backup singer kept warm just in case, it took center table as if it always expected to be on this stage. The family sang another round of ridicule before plates were served. My mother did her best to play along, but the dinner was burning her sheet music.

At a local Jamaican restaurant, I ordered ackee & saltfish with rice & peas instead of pairing it with boiled banana, yam, and dumpling. The woman behind the counter called me *yankee-bowy* and fixed my plate. Her reaction reheated leftovers I didn't know I had been carrying for years. There was something baked into her undertones I couldn't see until I visited Jamaica for the first time. When I landed in Montego Bay, the taxi driver spoke to me in patois while I looked out of the window. I thought about my grandparents and great grandparents as I tried to understand the hole in the airport's ceiling, the puddle on its bathroom floor, and the random goats on the road. The sights were characters from bedtimes stories I'd wished for but was never told. I rolled up one pant leg and both shirtsleeves. The reggae, soca, and occasional hip-hop on the radio accented the air like overlapping flags; this absorption back into the homeland became a halted fairytale at the resort's gates.

At the main entrance, a man sat in the sun manually operating a heavy barrier arm. He looked hot, dehydrated, and overworked. Next to him, another man patted down exiting employees; it was explained to me: if they get caught taking surplus food home instead of throwing it in the trash, they will be fired and blacklisted. The size and shape of the resort, combined with the treatment of the workers, made the environment seem too plantation-like for comfort. In the dining hall, a Black Jamaican man did the Bogle while balancing a cup on his head. At another table, three Black Jamaican men sang Bob Marley songs for tips. The experience got more painful by the spoonful. People abandoned full plates of food on tables and didn't look the workers in their eyes when they spoke. A Rasta got kicked out of the restaurant *for looking rough and making visitors feel uncomfortable.* On an upper deck, a Black comedian from a nineties television show sat with his blonde wife. I wanted to blame them for the yardman's removal, but there was no way to be sure they registered the complaint. As much as I hated to admit it, the dread was run off the premises out of consideration for all of the foreign tourists, myself included. I thought there was a significant distance between the Hollywood celebrity and myself, but from the right angle we looked the same. It didn't matter where my family was from. I was dressed in sneakers that could have been sold for $12,000 Jamaican dollars; and those were the ones I didn't mind getting dirty; the ones I purchased every few months because I was saving the unworn pairs already in my closet. I was embarrassed and wanted the staff to know I was different, but that's what everybody had been telling me the whole time. Regardless of where my family was from, I was laced with a privilege I didn't want anybody to see or acknowledge. In 2014, my sister invited me to hear a speech given by Stephen C. Vasciannie. At the time, he was the Jamaican ambassador to the United States. Following his address, we had a brief conversation. I told him about my visit to Jamaica and my family research projects. His response was, *I hope you find the peace you're looking for.* He was right; there were parts of myself I was trying to reconcile. My West Indian identity and practice of culture was informed in a much different way than my international friends' and relatives'. It was hyphenated by first-world advantages. The resort, the conversation with the ambassador, and the smirking woman at the restaurant reframed how my mother was treated at that family dinner. Even when I didn't have the words to explain, her feelings of rejection and humiliation were clear to me: that holiday gathering was a chance for her to perform a cultural ritual that would affirm her membership in our clan; the jokes turned it into a scarification ceremony. My family came from an island where freshwater was scarce, food insecurity was high, and the value of the Jamaican dollar was low; now they were in the United States, where there was enough food to experiment with recipes; spare pots of rice & peas could be prepared; and grandchildren could wear expensive sneakers while expecting special accommodations for breakfast. Ever since I touched the land my family left, I've thought about my grandparents and great-grandparents as children fantasizing themselves away from dirt roads and empty stomachs in Jamaica; sometimes I wonder if I were in their shoes and woke up in one of my wildest dreams, would I cry or laugh until it hurt.

When holiday dinners were no longer a family tradition, I decided to take the kitchen into my own hands. No matter how much I'd intellectualized rice & peas over the years, or how good my mother had gotten at making it, I still felt an inherited pressure when I prepared the ingredients. When it was time to cook, I played a lover's rock mixtape to control the anxiety. Also, to be safe, I made my own backup pots of rice: one had rice & peas, coconut milk, and a scotch bonnet pepper; another was just rice and peas; and a third was plain white rice boiled according to the directions on the Uncle Ben's box. In the middle of a Beres Hammond song, I headed to the store to buy gravy for the various rice dishes. When I returned with Heinz Turkey Gravy in a jar, the jokes opened and laughter poured. My grandparents and great-grandparents returned to us through the aromatics. They carried my eyes to the running water wasting down the drain. As I turned off the faucet, my mother offered to teach me about straining stock and browning flour.

We laughed about how getting recipes wrong might be a rite of passage in our family. When the lumps were gone from the gravy, there were still sweet potato pies to figure out. The last time I thought about making one, I gave up at the supermarket and purchased two premade pies. Buying individually wrapped pies from Crown Chicken might have been the better idea. The store brand pies were so bad my mother announced to the room: *You all will be happy to know, no actual sweet potatoes were harmed in the making of this pie.* I poured sorrel for everyone; I don't want to call the drink a secret weapon or a backup plan, but it was the right color, the sweet-to-tart ratio was balanced, and it saved me from the pie roasting. Over the drinks, we talked about buying land in Jamaica. None of us knew where to start. We were too many generations removed.

multitrack

The woman behind the counter called me yankee-bowy.

Mixdown

Kick drum: Customs agents don't care.

Snare: Your country was destabilized by the flag on their paychecks.

Bassline: Deportation comes with a jail cell.

Chords: I think this from a distance.

Vocal track: Jamaicans only hear my American accent.

    Reverb: They call me *Freshwater Yankee*.

      Reverb: They call me *Jamerican*.

        Reverb: They call me *Ja'fakin'*.

          Compression: Whenever they get a change.

Sample chop: They / they / don't / don't / do this to white people.
They / they / don't / don't / do this to white people.

Keys: . . . not even the ones with dreadlock wigs.

Strings: They know where the money is.

Vocal track: The first time I heard Spanish
it was spoken to my great-grandmother.

Vocal track: The first time I spoke Spanish a teacher graded me on it.

Vocal track: The last time I needed Spanish I had to think in English.

Background: Nobody told me about Jamaicans in Panama.

Background: Nobody told me about Jamaicans in Cuba.

Harmony: School taught Black history.

      Filter: They defund the Swahili teacher.

            Pan Left: Language is culture.

Pan Right: Culture is language.

      Compression: They want standard American.

Echo: This is how the world sees me.

Feedback: my birth certificate.

      Feedback: my passport.

Feedback: my accent.   **Feedback:** no fear of deportation.

    Mixdown: luxury.   **Mixdown:** privilege.

      Mixdown: distortion.

Cassette
Single

records in the front room

had   *stories*   *to talk about*

Electric Mayhem

Superhero pajamas and *Mork & Mindy* suspenders is how old we is.
Muppet Show on television is what time it is.
Good sofa by the glass table in the living room is where our mother is.
Unhinging the downstairs door is where our father is.
Revolver spring ready is where our stepfather is.
Neighbors too scared to do anything is where community is.
This is what it is is what they say it is
but what is to become of a stepson of a gun
if not adjusted to an estranged broken window
by electric mayhem o'clock?

Last Christmas

My father gift-wraps the airsoft
replica Ruger exactly how they were
before orange safety caps. It clicks in my hand
and sparks shoot out; my mother:
We don't play with guns
in this house. If you're from where I'm from,
you know what it means
when a Black mother takes something
and puts it up:

If you don't turn off that Nintendo
and take out that garbage
I'm going to take it
and put it up;

any more language like that in my house
I'm going to take those records
and put them up.

Put up means, if you know
where it is, you better not touch it
because what you get won't be
what you want.

It doesn't have bullets;
nobody is going to get hurt, I don't say
out loud; my arms swing, back-talk
to keep quiet: what does she know
about guns. She asks if I got something to say;
and I, yes, got something to say, but k/no/w
when a Black mother says, *you got something to say*
you better not got something to say
because rhetorical is a warning
best served unopened.

The subject is off the table;
it's out of my hands;
it's above me now;
younger than Tamir Rice when it is locked away,
older than John Crawford when it remains
out of the question. What does she know
about guns. The closet door closes
the snub nose on a shelf. In the dark
the airsoft answers, *everything.*

Clearing Clutter

Family Court ordered my father to meet me every other weekend for parental visitations. The arranged meetings were scheduled to take place at a neutral location: the Salvation Army's recreational center. The need for neutrality wasn't apparent to me until my mother had to file a restraining order against my father. I can't say I blame my mother for reaching out to the courts. Restraining orders are usually necessary when you suspect close distances will result in some sort of violence. I don't think my mother was worried about her safety. The problem was more between my father and my stepfather. Those men were far too oil-and-water to ever be civil in each other's presence. Neither of them was the type to back down from a fight. There was almost a shoot-out in our apartment's downstairs hallway once. I'm not sure about the politics behind the altercation—I don't want to speculate. What I do know is that my father was downstairs banging on the door and my mother didn't seem rattled. She told me to go into my room and close the door when we heard my stepfather say, . . . *oh if he comes in here, I got something for him.* With this warning in the air, he pulled our big red velvet chair in front of the apartment's door, sat down, and waited.

The entire neighborhood knew my stepfather carried guns. He used to call his revolver Roscoe and walk with it peeking out of his suit jacket. I'm not sure if my father carried guns or not. If he did, he kept them far away from my sight. He was a bodybuilder who used the word *rumble* when talking about fights. Eventually, the police arrived when the voices and banging got too chaotic for the neighbors. My father was arrested that evening. The next weekend, my mother explained that he was no longer allowed within a hundred feet of our house. None of this bothered me. In my neighborhood, going to jail didn't seem like a big deal. The next day somebody asked me how my father was. I remember my seven-year-old mouth saying, *he's in jail.* The words flowed with nonchalance, *where else would he be?*

The Salvation Army visits were embarrassing. Everybody knew that place was where dysfunctional fathers and sons were ordered to meet.

I didn't want to be seen walking in, and I didn't want people to judge my mother. I knew what people said and thought about inner-city single mothers back then. Words like *irresponsible* and *lack of education* always got thrown around carelessly. My mother was a multiple-college-degree-holding research scientist. Her focus was neuropsychology. The judgmental eyes I imagined watching us were blinded by assumptions. All they saw was a single Black woman and her son stepping out of a 1976 Buick Electra.

The funny thing about our Buick, sometimes the passenger side door flew open during turns. It happened so much my mother developed an automatic response. She never pulled over or stopped; she grabbed the door, slammed it closed, and kept it moving: no reduction of speed, nothing. I thought it was hilarious as long as it didn't happen on the way to the Salvation Army because what's funny on one block is embarrassing on the next.

I hated those mandatory trips to the Salvation Army. They made me feel like I needed to explain and justify my situation. Every meeting was supervised by a white social worker who made things uncomfortable. There was something about their voices when they told us about the fun we were going to have and how we should pretend they weren't in the room. We tried to ignore them, but they were too distracting with their note taking and clock watching. Also, we had to get their permission for everything. If we wanted to play basketball or pool, we had to ask. After those meetings I wondered if the social workers went home and talked about us over dinner. My father didn't like the way our visits were set up either. I believe he only agreed to them because he wanted to annoy my mother. His position became clear when, without a word about it, he simply stopped showing up.

I wasn't upset about his absence. I was more worried about sitting in that office with those social workers and their stock comfort phrases: *I'm really sure he wanted to be here; don't think his not being here means he doesn't love you; and you can talk to us—we're here to listen.* I knew there was no way they could be sure of what they were saying, but they were trained to know the right things to say. I wasn't trying to hear them. It would've felt better had they just played it straight and said, *he didn't show up, and that's messed up; do you want us to call your mother?* It would have been harsh, but it would have made it easier for me to take them seriously. By not doing so, they proved how much of my life they didn't understand.

What they didn't know was I had already seen my father ignore and walk past me on the street more than once. I went to his house a couple of times, but he pretended not to be home. I knew he was there because his neighbors told me they saw him upstairs. The next time we spoke, I asked if he heard me downstairs knocking. He didn't sugarcoat or lie to me. Without a blink, he said, *I knew you were down there. I just didn't feel like coming to the door.* I didn't give up on him until later visitation compromises failed. The last agreement was for him to pick me up every other weekend. He didn't follow through, and I got sick of waiting for him not to show up.

My mother and I used to see my father on the subway, and he would straight up look past us. We were nothing more than city clutter to him. I imagine how that must have made my mother feel. I never wanted to make her feel like she had to explain, so I tried not looking at either of them. She used to catch me glance at him and wouldn't say anything until I looked back at her. As soon as my attention returned, she would say his ignorance is his loss and tell me not to be like him when I'm grown. She spoke low enough to not cause a spectacle, but loud enough for him to hear. He would just sit there and let her voice get lost in the sound of the rocking train car. As I gained more independence, I started randomly seeing him downtown when my mother wasn't around. Once, I followed him for a few blocks. He pretended not to see me, but he knew I was behind him. He was a U.S. Marine. If he could tell when he was being followed in a jungle, a teenager tracking him down an empty street should have been easy to detect. It was there, on that street, when I decided never to speak to him again. During my sophomore year in high school, I saw him in a barbershop. We sat in opposite chairs, got haircuts, and I kept my word to myself.

I didn't see my father again until I was in college. We were in the supermarket. He stood two lanes away and wasn't alone. He held the hand of a small child. I didn't know what to say or think. The small boy could have been my younger cousin, brother, or something. I still don't know. The friend I was shopping with noticed shock on my face. He asked me what was wrong. I had to think of something. I pointed at the aisle and asked my friend if the man over there looked familiar. I should have been satisfied when he said no, but I wasn't. I told him that was my father. My friend's facial reaction reminded me of the social workers at the Salvation Army, but, unlike them, his concern and compassion felt real and without pity. It made me uncomfortable. If I could have run away, I would have. I didn't know what to do, so I pretended to be joking until he and the whole supermarket were behind me.

Around graduation time, I decided to give my father one more shot. I found his new apartment and stood for a long time at the end of his driveway until my emotions were in check enough to ring the bell. I was surprised when he answered and let me in the house. It was the middle of the night. His new family was asleep in the next room. I didn't want to disturb them, but it was too late—I'd already done that by showing up. We got around the small talk as I asked him why he stopped coming to our visits. After a beat, he said he was trying to wean me off him. I was more hurt than mad. I was looking for honesty and got it.

On the way out, I handed him a flier for an event I was DJ'ing that weekend. I told him his name would be on the guest list. He never showed up. I didn't see him again until years later. While working on my family research, I typed his name into Google. A picture of him in a gray Champion crewneck sweatshirt appeared. It was similar to one I had in my closet. A few weeks later, I threw mine away.

elders　　　*didn't tell*　　　*much*

　　　　　　　about our　　*journey*

Archeology

Aunt Betty's memory fades an almanac of family information. Her best efforts only recognize pictures of her eldest brother, father, mother, and son. Her nieces, nephews, sisters, and younger brother have all dissolved too far for recollection. Occasionally, she pulls a new name or location from the haze, but these recoveries can't always be sequenced properly. As history fragments, disconnects, and dissipates under her Alzheimer's, I turn her living room into an archeological dig. Questions become sifter trays and shovel; answers become uncovered relics preserved and archived. My computer screen introduces her to her grandparents for the first time. She finds out her grandmother's name was Charlotte; this pulls Aunt Betty's attention to the upper left corner of the room. Her mind has been triggered, so I wait for her to respond: *Sandra-Charlotte-Rose.* She sweeps the names together as if they are one. Two of the three I recognize—her youngest sister: Sandra, her grandmother: Charlotte— but Rose is unfamiliar. I repeat *Rose* back to her. She looks like she remembers a memory, but not the words that belong to it. This same confusion frustrated her into hand gestures when we talked about her father and she lost the syllables for cricket bat. The search for Rose makes her ask if we're in Canada. The activated memories, dust through her fingers, when I tell her we're in California. After securing our location, her mind migrates into a story about Grandma Sylvia, Jamaica, and Toronto. I wait for Aunt Betty to say Cuba, but she doesn't. There's a story there, I just can't get to it. President Obama eased some of the national restrictions blocking us, but the wall my family built still stands. When Aunt Betty returns, she says her mother lived in Canada with Aunt Rose. I never knew Grandma Sylvia had a sister Rose; this sends me to search for documents that might relate.

On my computer, I find a scanned copy of Grandma Sylvia's wedding certificate. On the right side of the image, in a space designated for witnesses, Rose appears. She is hard to pull from the cursive, but her identity straightens out and becomes more legible the harder I look. I wonder who else is lost in the margins. Rose's husband is also there, but his name is too smeared in ink for me to recover him. Deciphering the names from aged artifacts gives Aunt Betty time to redirect toward an old boyfriend in New York, a foster son from Africa, and her time in the military. She grabs a picture from a stack on the table and new artifacts are unearthed. She climbs in the photo and finds herself back on the island. Her sisters are there, but she doesn't say their names, and I can't see them. Between Aunt Betty and what might be a village, a boat floats past. We don't know who is on it or where it goes. The land behind her is too out of focus for naming so we just accept the shape it takes in the backdrop. Her smile makes me promise to find the people and places that still make her this happy. Conversations like this usually stop before my curiosity wanders too deep into Jamaica. Today, there is no subject change. Maybe she is ready for me to find something. I don't know, but I can tell the search is exhausting her. I save my notes and close the open documents on the desktop. She watches the computer power down, ending our excavation. When the screen goes black, she looks back at the snapshot in her hand, and says, *tell them that I was smiling because they were taking my picture.*

Lepidopterist

Kingston ends when the Rasta tells me
everything I'm looking for is looking
for me. The van between parishes, a pilgrimage
through the archive. I've imagined this landscape:
ackee trees, breadfruit trees, mango trees, family
roots. I've never found any living in Jamaica, but today I am
a butterfly net determined to catch a fluttering mythology. In Mandeville
I speak birth certificates over a phone, and my accent crawls
back to New York. Its version of Jamaican patois returns
to a shelf next to recipes, photographs, and other chipped statuettes
I'm here to reassemble. The next day
a computer search surrenders a death certificate
with an address. I find a house caged in
a patient revelation. A woman opens
the door, speaks in kaleidoscopes, and hands
over a swallowtail. She points toward the city.
It flies. I follow. It becomes a cousin. We meet
for the first time. It rains as we hug
like a fork in the road bent back on itself.

Trademarks

The embargo split us before our parents were born
on opposite sides of a missile crisis. His grandfather lost English
on the way to Havana. I picked up Spanish, but it falls
under pressure. At the table after the lunch table
he finds a bed at the bottom of a beer bottle and runs from it
back to the family reunion: our grandparents were cousins
now they are dead
conversations that can't be reintroduced
because the translator is in the bathroom
or walking back
or far enough to see our native tongues are not indigenous
to our bodies, they are proofs of purchase replicating
on autopilot, auction-block fugitives pledging allegiance
to the branding iron, they are African
voice boxes crushed into blood diamonds bought and sold
on the black market. No matter how far from the plantation
my cousin and I still aren't free. We can't even speak
without a master of both present
to translate our trademarks.

Photosynthesis

The photo album, a museum, we search for lives
fallen out of touch; on the gallery floor, an exhibit
we trace against folklore; we think we know
something about Jamaica, so we think
we know something about this tableau
pressed between plastic and the context it falls from.
It self-identifies Panama; and it is
inscribed to Aunt Betty. She remembers nothing. Age paints over
her and everything she has ever seen
she now sees for the first time every time
she sees it again. The signature claims itself
her cousin. I take its word for it. She takes mine
but forgets. In Brazil, a woman loses her grandfather.
She doesn't know we find him
because we are too far

                         in the future.

I re/search the image and social-media rabbit-holes
over the years and distance. We find again the man we could not
place. At a wedding with his granddaughter
he looks at me
through the picture; I reach out; she sees me
and reaches back.

Architect

The death certificate says *occupation: planter*; this makes me think I know everything I need to know. I fight my imagination not to recreate the big house, fields, and enslaved people, but it's not easy. The last time I saw the word *plantation* posted on something was in Bristol, England; that entire day was spent being confused by a street named *Whiteladies Road*. Everybody tried to explain the street's name and how it wasn't racist, but none of it made sense. The upper portion of the street was called *Blackboy Hill*. People told me how that wasn't racist either. I knew there was no way to understand these streets without exploring them for myself.

As I walked around the city, I ended up in front of a Caribbean restaurant called, you guessed it, *Plantation*. I asked the manager, who was not Black, if he saw anything wrong with the restaurant's name; he looked as if he had never been asked that question before. Black men in the kitchen, interested in our conversation, peeked through the door. My voice raised enough for them to hear but not enough for the police to be called. Retelling this story lays the foundation of the big house in my mind. The manager, white and annoyed, asked if I wanted a menu. I said, no. Instead, I waved the Black-power-fist at the men in the kitchen, and walked out. People throughout the city, Black and otherwise, also excused the restaurant's name while explaining how another place with a sign that read *Nappy Laundry* wasn't what I thought it was. After talking culture, language, and pluralism with more random strangers, it was decided: *I was being too American.* Now here I am, an American back in America, reading a Jamaican death certificate, and trying to understand an eighty-year-old plantation owner from the distance of 90 years in the future. The microfilm is as English as that restaurant's name and those street signs. It says his name was Richard; he was my great-grandmother's father, and he died from apoplexy.

On the way back from looking up *apoplexy*, I get pulled into a website that lists Richard's children. The site tells me my Grandma Sylvia had a brother named Oscar. Other siblings are listed, but I focus on him because his age, gender, and the mechanics of patriarchy make him easier to trace over generations. The internet search explains that he moved from Jamaica to Central America for work. When I was young and busy minding grown folks' business, I had heard stories about our family traveling between Jamaica and Panama. There was even a picture of a Panamanian man named Vicente. I have the photo now, but not the story behind it. The signature says *A mi prima Betty*. I tried talking to my aunt about this, but she doesn't remember much. During this research session in the National Archive, Oscar is the answer to many questions. I know he was Black because the ink that calls him a Negro is clear. The phrasing of his race erects the frame and trusses for the big house that I try to not reconstruct.

Another internet search reveals a Panamanian man who claims Oscar as his great-grandfather. After cross-referencing his Twitter with Instagram and Facebook, I land on a picture of Oscar's son and grandson, both named Vicente. I send the Twitter user, and his father, a message, but neither respond. I think they must have looked at my profile and decided that I was a computer scammer. For my next attempt, I figure it is better to be vague and public. I look through their pictures until I find an appropriate comment section to insert my voice. The perfect opportunity is found on an Instagram page belonging to a Panamanian woman living in Brazil. She is the cousin of the original Twitter user. The caption identifies Vicente as her grandfather. I want to contact her by direct message, but I don't want her to think that I'm trying to slide in her DMs. I stick with the original plan: vague and public. Under the photo, I comment: *I know the man in the picture.* I can tell that she loves and misses Vicente too much not to respond. In a matter of minutes, she does; I introduce myself and explain how our grandparents might have been cousins. I can tell she wants to believe me, but the Spanish, Portuguese, and English between us make it difficult.

She remembers hearing about Jamaica when she was young, but always understood her great-grandfather to have been British. When she tells me this I wonder if she means white, but I don't ask. The uncertainty secures walls and a roof on the big house. I ignore the painting and hammering, and explain how she is right; Richard, Sylvia, and Oscar were British because they were born in Jamaica before 1962. She doesn't identify as Black and told me it's considered racist for her to use the word *favela* instead of *community* in Brazil. She says that word is only said by people who live in that area. I understand because we have words only my community is allowed to use. I ask if she is surprised that she might have a _____ cousin in New York. I pause on Black, but she knows what I mean and says her family is *international* and nothing surprises her. This makes me want to check the support beams on the big house, but I don't. Instead, I expose the family picture; she makes a positive identification; we agree to Skype, and construction slows for the day.

Algorithm

for the white friend left in São Paulo

4) Your Black friend plans to explore Blackness on an international scale by finding and interviewing ten cousins in ten different countries. Agree to photo document the journey. He will pay for flights and housing. When the first flight lands in São Paulo, leave your Black friend on the plane. Never mind how good home training says: wait for your entire party at the end of the jet bridge. You are to leave the gate alone, clear customs, and wait for your suitcases because you travel with more baggage than necessary.

8) Between the airport and Airbnb, Brazilian music will be explained through the lens of African religions. The conversation will reach the difference between race, nationality, and ethnicity. When you realize Brazilian isn't a race, struggle to understand Black and Latino not being mutually exclusive. Be confused when you can't guess who is, or isn't, Black during the taxi ride.

10) Think you can say whatever you want. Forget you're not home, or forget everywhere isn't your home. Do, to this conversation, what you helped do to Bushwick: center yourself in it, then when affected people resist, take your shirt off; sweat on the furniture; put your feet up; open your computer; quote the time Tony Soprano said N_____. Get angry when your Black friend walks out. Say you aren't racist because you lived with two Black women, and because you haven't said that word in ten years.

5) Ask why Black people still worship white religions? Say it was illegal for Black people to practice their own religions, but this changed; it was illegal for them to read, but they fought and that changed. Don't think about how you're asking for a whites-only space in religion. Ignore how racism impacts literacy rates in Black communities. Talk about the civil rights movement. Dismiss resistance movements started in, or housed by, Black churches. Talk about how you respect Martin Luther King Jr. more than Malcolm X. Say: *There is something noble about Black people not fighting back.* Mention Dr. King again. Forget he was a reverend in a Black church. Say: *Exploration is beautiful, and white kids should be able to touch a Black girl's hair without being called racist.* Forget Black women aren't all-inclusive vacation packages. Just enjoy excursions through their discomfort. Sip your frozen entitlement by the beach. Disregard the lifeguards and demand your children be allowed to swim the off-limits, towel off, and go home guilt-free.

6) Express frustration with movies depicting white teachers helping Black kids in Black communities. From here, lead into a discussion about a movie you're writing. Let the premise be a depressed Black basketball player who can only recapture inner joy by coaching white kids at a private school on Manhattan's Upper East Side. When your Black friend points out how your film imagines Black happiness as a reward granted through the servitude of white people, argue. Say: *White kids have problems too.* Demand freedom for white people to make art about Black people without restriction.

7) Feel offended when the Black friend offers an article about racial sensitivity, and say: *No, I don't want to because it feels like you're telling me I need to read some sh*!.*

3) Everything is out of order: you, your behavior, and the need for this instruction manual. If disorientation gets too overwhelming, repeat step 10.

2) Have a Black friend you're willing to lose.

1) Don't apologize.

Crossfader

entries and images date back to the 1800s

in   This inheritance

Photo Shoot

Today, a photographer focuses on discolored bricks, wooden doors, and a banister that partially hides two men and one woman. There are men on the concrete stairs and on the stained sidewalk. They, like the men on the porch, are dressed in suits; some wear clerical collars and medals on their jackets. In front of the building, and all of the people, is Louise. We met her yesterday. Her husband, our great-grandfather, stands over her left shoulder; her brother-in-law is over her right. Her hair is black and pinned. Her shoes coordinate with her coat. Serious and proud, she looks into the camera like her name has the power of an entire church behind it.

Tomorrow, you will be at your grandmother's house trying to be quiet because you will know, like I already know, she won't like people making noise during her stories. Between commercial breaks, she will realize the grandson she describes as rambunctious is being too quiet. She will tell you, from her bedroom, *don't be downstairs rummaging through stuff*, because you will be, downstairs, rummaging through stuff until you find a picture printed on thick cardstock. You will only recognize your great-grandmother in the picture. You could learn your great-great-grandparents' names. One of them might be in the photograph. You should ask your grandmother about what you've found, but you won't. Instead of appreciating this photo archive, draw on it with pens and crayons, put it back in the cabinet, and forget about it.

Tomorrow, encounter this picture in your adulthood. Notice, crayon and pen marks—how you scribbled yourself into its timeline; focus on the jagged edges and missing sections—when you scan it with your eyes, with your fingers, with your computer. Trace photographic element until you land on the unidentified white man in the picture. Look at his face, then at your great-grandmother, and wonder if that's her father. Consider what anti-miscegenation laws did for their choice of Bermuda over the United States when they left Jamaica. They died between Pace v. Alabama and Loving v. Virginia. Think about how there is still a little old-time Alabama and Virginia in every city hall; you can see it in the citizens. Remember every time you walked with a woman who was not Black at first glance—how the sneers and whispers echoed through you long after they were gone.

Between today and tomorrow, your grandmother gets married and moves to the United States. Forty years before a firebomb turns his church into rubble and cinder, your great-grandfather dies in a traffic accident. Your great-grandmother remarries and is lost in time. Her grandchildren remember everything you will have to imagine. You should ask our grandmother about her mother while you have the chance.

Between tomorrow and tomorrow, the burning church clears into luxury apartments. Ten years away, a different church is named after your great-grandfather's brother. Keys to its location are in the picture you've forgotten. As its cardstock deteriorates in a cabinet, you and your friends take pictures with Kid Capri outside of a Canadian nightclub. You feel like you've been here before but don't know how to explain it. As fast as the camera snaps, this moment becomes a lost photo. Fifteen years from now, ask a friend if he still has a copy. When he says no, continue tracking your great-grandparents through time. You will find them when you look at birth certificates, newspaper articles, and the ship manifests.

Dear Louise;

If obituaries are worth their weight in tombstones
        stress poured your mother from her body.

If newspapers are worth their weight in horror
        she saw your father kill Africans for the crown.

If military records are worth their weight in segregation
        his rank was white and officer.

If one-drop-rule is worth its weight in racism
        your mother will keep us.

If sermon is worth its weight in asylum
        your husband was a sanctuary.

If cut brake lines are worth their weight in sniper rifles
        he was assassinated by a traffic stop.

If echoes are worth their weight in helix codes
        raise your daughter to raise my mother to raise me
        on oxtail soup, eucalyptus oil, and insight
        to see there is still a war against Africans.

If debt is worth its weight in weapons
        the IMF planted landmines through Jamaica
        and poverty exploded.

If sabotage is worth its weight in intervention
          after you die, be a malfunctioning canister
          refusing to tear gas our uprisings
          over African schoolgirls gone missing
          over playground slides into prison yards
          over food deserts
          over corroded water
          over housing crisis
          over healthcare costing body parts

          we you can't afford to lose.

If proof is worth its weight in patterns
          there is still a war against Africans
          we've been fighting as long as you
          can remember.

The Book of Alice

1:1 *There was a* ~~man~~ *woman in* ~~the land of Uz~~ *the state of* New York, *whose name was* ~~Job~~ Alice; *and that* ~~man~~*-woman was perfect and upright, and one that feared God, and eschewed evil.*

1:2 *And there were born unto* ~~him~~ *her* ~~seven~~ *three sons, and* ~~three~~ *two daughters: one alive and one returned.*

1:3 ~~His~~ *Her substance also was* ~~seven thousand sheep~~ *a good name in the* neighborhood, ~~and three thousand camels~~ *an oxtail soup recipe,* ~~and five hundred yoke of oxen~~ *a bottle of eucalyptus oil,* ~~and five hundred she asses~~ hundreds of family pictures and stories, *and a very great household; so that this* ~~man~~ *woman was the greatest of all the* ~~men~~ *women of the east.*

1:4 *And* ~~his sons~~ *her daughter held occasional holiday dinners at her* ~~went and feasted in their houses,~~ house, ~~every one his day;~~ *and sent and called for* ~~their three sisters~~ *her mother and siblings* ~~to eat and to drink with them~~ *her.*

1:5 *And it was so, when the day of their feasting was done,* ~~Job~~ Alice *sent* ~~and sanctified them, and rose up early in the morning, and~~ *prayer* ~~offered burnt~~ *offerings according to the number of them all: for* ~~Job~~ Alice *said, it may be that my* ~~sons~~ *children have sinned,* ~~and cursed God in their hearts~~*. Thus did* ~~Job~~ Alice *continually.*

1:6 *Now there was a day when the sons of God came to present themselves before the LORD, and Satan came also among them.*

1:7 *And the LORD said unto Satan, Whence comest thou? Then Satan answered the LORD, and said, from going to and fro in the earth, and from walking up and down in it.*

1:8 And the LORD said unto Satan, Hast thou considered my servant ~~Job~~ Alice, *that there is none like ~~him~~ her in the earth, a perfect and an upright ~~man~~ woman, one that feareth God, and escheweth evil?*

1:9 Then Satan answered the LORD, and said, Doth ~~Job~~ Alice fear God for nought?

1:10 Hast not thou made a hedge about ~~him~~ Alice, and about ~~his~~ her house, and about all that ~~he~~ she hath on every side? Thou hast blessed the work of ~~his~~ her ~~hands~~ heart, and ~~his~~ her substance is increased in the land.

1:11 But put forth thine hand now, and touch all that ~~he~~ she hath, and ~~he~~ she *will curse thee to thy face.*

1:12 And the LORD said unto Satan, Behold, all that ~~he~~ she hath is in thy power; only upon ~~himself~~ herself put not forth thine hand. So Satan went forth from the presence of the LORD.

1:13 And there was a day when ~~his~~ her youngest sons and ~~his daughters~~ daughter *were eating and drinking wine in their ~~eldest brother's house~~* houses.

1:14 And there came a messenger unto ~~Job~~ Alice, and said, ~~The oxen were plowing, and the asses feeding beside them~~: Your husband made pregnant another woman.

1:15 And the ~~Sabeans~~ AIDS plague fell upon ~~them~~ her son, the messenger said~~; and took them away.; yea, they have slain the servants with the edge of the sword; and I only am escaped alone to tell thee.~~

1:16 While he was yet speaking, there came also another, and said, ~~The fire of God is fallen from heaven, and hath burned up the sheep, and the servants, and consumed them~~ cancer has killed your husband.~~; and I only am escaped alone to tell thee.~~

1:17 While he was yet speaking, there came also another, and said, ~~The Chaldeans made out three bands, and fell upon the camels, and have carried them away, yea, and slain the servants with the edge of the sword; and I only am escaped alone to tell thee.~~ The plague has killed your son.

1:18 While he was yet speaking, there came also another, and said, ~~Thy sons and thy daughters were eating and drinking wine in their eldest brother's house:~~ Diabetes has come to take your legs as it did your grandfather's.

1:19 And, behold, there came a great wind from the wilderness, and smote the ~~four corners of the house, and it fell upon the young men, and they are dead; and I only am escaped alone to tell thee.~~ relationship between mother, daughter, and granddaughter.

1:20 Then ~~Job~~ *Alice arose,* ~~and rent his mantle, and shaved his head, and fell down upon the ground, and worshipped,~~ in a nursing home alone.

1:21 And said, Naked came I out of my mother's womb, and naked shall I return thither: the LORD gave, and the LORD hath taken away; blessed be the name of the LORD.

1:22 In all this ~~Job~~ *Alice sinned not, nor charged God foolishly.*

Turntables

uncles remember

noses would bleed

if he looked at them

Cue Point: 2008

Skip never took me to play cricket, nothing. We didn't even speak when we passed each other in the hallway. My mother used to ask if we spoke. We'd be like, no, he ain't speak to us. First of all, . . .

Backspin

In the backyard, a brindle Pit named Sexy and a Rottweiler puppy named Bear. Parked in front, a gold Mazda RX-7. In the bedroom, a complicated entertainment system: dual tape decks, reel-to-reel, record players, speakers, and amplifiers. Also hooked up to this system, a VCR and a color television. We're talking some serious technology for the time. Let's be clear, a new VCR could cost up to $250. This is a lot of money considering the current minimum wage is only $3.35. Think about it, at the end of a five-day week, a full-time worker could come home with $134 before taxes, rent, or any other bills. Let's consider the inflation rate: according to the Department of Labor, $250 in 1989 is the same as $635.40 in 2023. If that's too much math, understand it this way: VCRs were expensive and this model came with a remote control. I mean, the remote does have a cord that needs to be plugged into the unit, so you could only be about three feet away when using it, but it has one and that increases the value.

Unnoticed in this room is a Gemini MX-2200 mixer. It's the exact same model DJ Jazzy Jeff uses. I'm not sure why I don't see it; mirrors cover most of the walls. Whatever isn't in my direct sight line should be visible through a reflection. There are also corkboards with pictures. I'm in some of them, my sister is in one, and my cousins are in others. There's even a photo of him, the Mayor, smoking in his army uniform. I'm not sure if he got that nickname before or after the photo was taken. On one shelf, there's a collection of non-prescription glasses; on another, some snapback hats are arranged. He sits on a tall chair dressed in a gray Chanel sweatshirt, jeans, and a pair of black Nike Cortez. On his waterbed, in a *Do the Right Thing* sweatshirt, jeans, and white Avia sneakers, I sit.

The Nintendo I purchased is hooked up and we're playing. It took a summer of dog walking and layaway payments, but I finally upgraded from the ColecoVision and Atari. This game system is the fifth thing I ever purchased for myself. The second, third, and fourth were rap albums: *By All Means Necessary* by BDP, *Lyte as a Rock* by MC Lyte, and *Long Live the Kane* by Big Daddy Kane; in that order. The first thing was the portable cassette player clipped to my belt. I bought it from him in this very bedroom. This tape player is 1980s-style fresh: it has a fast-forward, a rewind, and an auto-reverse button. This ain't no normal silver Walkman with orange sponge headphones. We're talking next level here. I remember the day he sold it to me. After I asked if I could borrow it several times, he said: *look, you can't be expecting people to just be giving you stuff whenever you ask. We don't do the handout thing over here. If you want something, you work for it. We work for everything we got. If you want this Walkman, you can buy it from me. Now, I know you ain't got no real ducats so I'll sell it to you for five bucks. You can make payments if you need to.* I agreed, and he handed it to me. Later that day, he sent me to the store for Phillies. He knew I wasn't old enough to buy tobacco products so he gave me a very easy script to follow. All I had to do was walk into the store and say: *yo was'sup, I need two for The Blunt Man.* We've done this before. It always worked. When I got back from the store, he told me keep the change. For about an hour, I debated spending the money but ended up giving it back to him as my first payment. He laughed and said, *good job.*

Now here we are, playing Double Dribble on the Nintendo I bought with my own money. I'm twenty points up and laughing because we know this video game is the only way I can beat him in basketball. In real life, he makes shots from anywhere on the court, but we aren't in a gym. We're in his room, he is getting dunked on every minute, and he can't take it. He smirks, cuts his eyes at me, growls my name, and laughs. Part of me thinks about slowing the dunk-a-thon down, but this is Double Dribble and the dunks are the most exciting part of the game. The players, the court, and the sounds are basic even by 8-bit graphic standards, but the dunks, the dunks look like a completely different design team created them.

From the chair, he tells me about the army friend who threatened to blow up the mess hall with a hand grenade, how he almost got court marshaled, how he got stranded in Phoenix, and how he thinks the family blames him for my grandfather leaving. In the next room, Nana watches *General Hospital*. She loves that show, Saratoga cigarettes, Kit Kats, Halls cough drops, maple walnut ice cream, and Stevie Wonder. She makes the best oxtail soup in the world, and I'm not just saying this because she is my grandmother. I don't yet know she will take the recipe with her. I can't imagine her gone.

On the reel-to-reel, a new jack swing mix plays so many good songs that will be forgotten over the next few years. People will remember BBD, Teddy Riley & Guy, Bobby Brown, Al B. Sure!, Janet Jackson, Keith Sweat, Father MC, and Redhead Kingpin. We're talking about artists who pop culture won't even remember as musicians. Tisha Campbell will probably end up more famous for her future roles as Gina on *Martin* and Sidney in *House Party*. Jasmine Guy will more likely be remembered as Whitley Gilbert from *A Different World*. Both women have new jack swing songs. Tisha has "Push" and Jasmine has "Try Me." I hear them on this mix, but as fast as their voices are introduced, their words trail from the instruments, the beat blends into another song, and another song, and another song, and I still don't notice the Gemini MX-2200 mixer hidden in the room. Today isn't the day I become a DJ, but it plugs in the framework. The connections make all of the displays light up. You can see it on my face.

Cue Point: 2010

Skip never took me to play cricket, nothing. We didn't even speak when we passed each other in the hallway. My mother used to ask if we spoke. We'd be like, no, he ain't speak to us. **First of all, we was scared of him. One time, we was supposed to ask him for school clothes, but I was the only one who spoke up. He looked at my mother and said:** . . .

The Mayor Be Like

Ain't nobody trying to buy no used car
- only one window work
- rearview mirrors got a crack
- back left tire flat
- cigarette butts all up in the ashtray
- coat hanger where the antenna supposed to be
- trunk got a bungee cord rope holding it closed
- inside smell like Aqua Velva;

                              Aqua Velva smell like drugstore.

Don't nobody want no used car smelling like no drugstore.
Drugstores sell A+D ointment and lottery tickets
at the same time.

Plus, what you look like buying a car
- one seat got a rip in it
- glove compartment won't stay closed
- headlight work when it want to
- air condition work when it want to
- radio work when it want to
- muffler drag on the ground and make all kinds of noise

How you buying a car and it sound like it's going faster than it is
even when it's stopped at a red light
- gotta shift into neutral so the engine don't cut off
- gotta pump the gas in neutral so the engine don't cut off
- gotta ride around with booster cable just in case the engine cut off

Don't nobody got time to be on no side of the road with no booster cables.

Booster cables is dangerous: sparks flying all over the place.
Plus, tow-truck drivers be talking about
- distributor cap
- alternator
- timing belt

Don't nobody know about no timing belt
and if they do know, they know don't nobody want no broken one
but this is how it goes. The market is risky
- new cars, shiny, people try to steal them
- old cars, classic, people try to steal them
- broken cars, fix'em, people try to steal them

and this ain't even about what you can fix.
It's about knowing what you can't
because time is an investment
               is a commitment
               is a relationship
and don't nobody need this many red flags
if they know they ain't no mechanic.

Cue Point: 2012

Skip never took me to play cricket, nothing. We didn't even speak when we passed each other in the hallway. My mother used to ask if we spoke. We'd be like, no, he ain't speak to us. First of all, we was scared of him. One time, we was supposed to ask him for school clothes, but I was the only one who spoke up. He looked at my mother and said: Are you going to let these children speak to me like this? Then . . .

One in the Chamber

When I talk to male friends or men in my family, we end up bonding over stories about fights we've won or lost. Regardless of where we start, there will be a laughter-filled reenactment of somebody being beaten up. We spend hours trying to one-up all of the times we've squared off in bars, streets, or parties. I used to think this was how we celebrated survival, and it might have been. It could have also been us not knowing how to connect and understand each other through any lens other than violence. It's hard to identify when we learned this, but we must have picked it up somewhere between patty-cake and slap-boxing.

In *We Real Cool: Black Men and Masculinity*, bell hooks discusses how violent experiences at an early age not only prepare us to perform violence but also teach us to be valued for our abilities to inflict harm. Reminiscing over our knuckle scars might have been our way to affirm our worth to each other. We were raised in a culture where violence as a service is a love language. We don't think about how thrown blows destroy us regardless of our relationship to the fists.

To the trained eye, my grandfather's resting face was a confident dare to anybody who wanted a problem. My uncles were so afraid of him, their noses bled when he looked at them too hard. Imagine being so scared of a parent your stress level draws blood from your body. What they survived as boys brings new light to the fight stories they tell as men. Love, loyalty, and compassion for them never let me ask what turned my grandfather, their father, into the man they remembered. At one point, he was my great-grandmother's baby; at another, he was a terrifying legend in a mean suit. As I grow, the generation gaps between us widen, and I see their lives in context. Masculinity wasn't openly considered a spectrum when they were children. My grandfather experienced violence at home, fought in World War II, and became a parent before post-traumatic stress disorder was common vocabulary. Therapy wasn't remotely accessible or socially acceptable for the average Black person at the time; it barely is now. I'm sure my grandfather and his friends shared bonding sessions similar to the ones I experience, but what if he had a professional to help him discuss trauma without the intention of preserving and repurposing the violence. He, like so many of us, was socialized to find pride and comfort in rage. There was a time when my father and stepfather threatened to kill each other. As clear as that moment is for me, I don't remember being scared. In retrospect, I think my mother hypnotized my stepfather to keep him seated. He could have drawn his gun and shot through the door, but he didn't. Every time I ask her if hypnosis was involved, she neither confirms nor denies. She just says there was no way she could have let him shoot my father in front of me. This and other violent situations most definitely contributed to my triggers.

In high school, a man tried to steal my mother's car out of our driveway. This was a third attempt at taking it. When I saw him jimmying the lock, I was walking our dog. She was a Rottweiler puppy who was limping after having been hit by a car a month before. Quietly, I took her in the house and grabbed the machete I inherited from my grandfather. When the thief saw me, he ran. I chased him into a neighbor's backyard. We fought and signaled for help at the top of our lungs. In the tussle, he tried to stab me with a screwdriver. It didn't occur to me I could have died in the middle of that impulse. Calling the police never entered my mind. All I could think about was how proud my uncles would be once I told them what happened.

Cue Point: 2014

Skip never took me to play cricket, nothing. We didn't even speak when we passed each other in the hallway. My mother used to ask if we spoke. We'd be like, no, he ain't speak to us. First of all, we was scared of him. One time, we was supposed to ask him for school clothes, but I was the only one who spoke up. He looked at my mother and said: Are you going to let these children speak to me like this? Then **he moved out. Everybody blames me for running him off. He hated me until the day he died. I found a note he wrote to my brother. He said he loved him. I ain't get no letter. Why he ain't love me?**

—**Mayor**

Records

Pops

        scratches

              and skips in the grooves

told back. Like music

        on vinyl

45 rpm

For the record, unsettled stone
split earthquakes into my grandfather.

For the record, cracks continued to open
fault lines through my family.

For the record, there was a cricket match.

For the record, there were strikes.

For the record, the aftershocks
made my grandfather
Skip.

33 1/3 rpm

Name

                    turned serial
                    turned number
                    turned orders
                    turned post
                    turned traumatic
                    turned mortar
                    turned expended
                    turned civilian
                    turned

detonation

Sunday 24-84

My dear Number one

son, I want to thank you so
much for the gift. It is beautiful. I love
it. Honey you are my number one son and I can
now say a son in whom I am very proud you
have made me so proud of you. I thank the
father above for you and all my children. My
one regret is that because of our economic
situation of these years. I did not grow up
with you all. I had to work shifts that kept
me away from you. I wont blame it all on that
I truly regret not growing up with you.
However I hope it is not too late to know my
children I am trying. Everyone here is ok
and send their love. Again my son I love
you very much and am proud of you. Hope to
see or hear from you.

I remain
your

Old man
Skip

78 rpm

The rhythm was West Indian calligraphy
was border crossing ambition
was pool hall trick shot
was clean suit church pew
was pinstripe and whitewall
was leather strap discipline
was back pocket wedding ring
was suicide cigarette
was dissipating echo
and still never a bad word out of my grandmother's mouth

maxi
single

Summer camp extended

beyond day
trips and Styrofoam lunch trays

Acrobatic

w/Uncle Danny

The summer you learn back handsprings
your uncle flips Marcus Garvey Park into theatre camp.
The stage is before chopped cheese attracts tour buses.
Costumes are from a Canal Street shopping spree
predating Chinatown somersaulting art galleries;
the script, just as absurd
as a pack of African American Ninjas
written into a dice game
rolled into a gang fight resolved by a dance-off
and sing-along; the piano, a gift wheeled
from a dying classroom that will be replaced
by loft apartments; still bouncing sideways
down the sidewalk, you see street vendors
and sneaker stores
and not the Starbucks on the way;
when it arrives, it sits on the corner as if it's been there
the whole time; it says, *few things survive this decade*
your uncle wasn't one of them.

Stable Flare

Pavement turns into gravel and then grass as gradually as the radio station drops from Rebbie Jackson and The Pointer Sisters into static. Lampposts and telephone wires become trees and branches on the side of the road. We try to let go of the nervousness, but it is playing at a high level. There is no controlling its volume as the surrendering a skyline lowers from the back window. We park, unpack, and a white man with torn jeans introduces himself as Camp-Counselor-Dent. Your mother notices what you've already picked up: you're the other Black kid moving in today. In every similar situation there always ends up being a fight. This camp will be no different, but this isn't where it happens.

Your cabin has one central light and no locks on the door. Think about a fire and claim the top bunk closest to the exit because it is window level. Also, home invaders usually use back doors, basements, or windows. If they kick in your front door, they might kill you. If they take the time to top pick the lock, then they probably think you're not home. They'll most likely enter slow to see if there is an alarm or a dog. When the coast is clear, they'll speed up, grab what they're looking for, and jet. This cabin has small windows, no basement, or back door. Watch the front door. If someone comes, hope they sneak past you, grab whatever they can pawn from Dent's side of the room, and run out. If they don't, you can slip through the window or run out of the open door. Remember it's small but not that small. Let this be sound logic until you read about the Girl Scouts in Oklahoma. The cabin where they stayed, and the path where they were found, probably looked similar to the scene you're standing in.

The other Black kid selects the bunk in the back of the cabin. You don't understand why. He probably doesn't know about Oklahoma either. Dent explains that beds have to be made, clothes have to be put away, and there will be daily inspections. There are no lockers, hampers, or washing machines. You have questions, but don't ask. Your cabinmates comment on your height. You've been measured like this before, but this isn't where the fight happens.

We exit the cabin and head toward the dining hall. Dent points out the communal bathroom while picking berries from trees and singing camp songs you've never heard before. You'll learn the words and sing along eventually. There are no cool tables in the dining hall like at school. Everybody here stays with their assigned groups. You notice a Black girl at another table, but you aren't paying her much attention because you've just figured out *bug-juice* is Kool-Aid; also, your table is talking about Transformers, G.I. Joe, and WWF. Girls vs. violent toys, cartoons, and wrestling is still a tough decision in the fourth grade. Dent asks if any of your parents paid extra for horseback riding lessons; you raise your hand; Dent puts a mark by your name and explains how he'll walk you to the stables tomorrow.

The next morning, you find out airhorns are the way they'll wake you up every day. You and the other campers run from your beds, across the courtyard, and into the bathroom. Every camper is in there at once. Very few guys take showers; the ones who do shower take them in their underwear. In a few weeks, white kids will be comfortable enough to comment on your dark skin and how they can't see your tan lines. There will be camp fights, but the first one isn't here, so you brush your teeth and run back to the cabin where Dent is popping face acne in the mirror. Growler, the head counselor, uses an animal-themed system to publicly announce our group's cleanliness scores in the middle of the courtyard. Swamp crane is our ranking for today. According to Growler, this is the worst. You tell your cabinmates this is the last swamp crane we're getting. They don't know how serious you are. You remind them again before you head to the stables.

You've never seen a horse up close. The first thing you notice is they're huge and stink. Morgan, the horseback-riding counselor, explains that we cannot let horses eat grass or drink from ponds during rides; we should not scream if a horse steps on our foot. You try to pay attention, but your eyes start to feel irritated. The counselors don't know how serious your allergies are, and you really want to ride the horses, so you try to rub the burning away. You notice Morgan always speaks to you last. She also puts her hands on her knees and takes deep breaths between words when addressing you. It becomes the most obvious when she leans in and says she has a special horse for you, his name is Cadillac. She smirks through the syllables in his name, and her co-counselors laugh. You know a stereotype when you hear one. You're embarrassed because your mother dropped you off in a yellow Seville, and your grandfather has a black Coupe de Ville. Your watering eyes swell shut, and your lungs close. The counselors see something is wrong, but it's too late. You're already in the saddle. The environment feels like it is trying to kill you, but this isn't where the fight happens. This is where you learn double consciousness is a reaction to an assault on your senses; also, racism is sometimes microbial—but invisible doesn't mean intangible. Prejudice is in the air, but you don't know what to do because adults put it there. Your swollen eyes and wheezing lungs try convincing you to retreat, but you don't know if it's safe to tell the counselors how Cadillac is making you feel. Morgan continues introducing you to Cadillac the exact same way for two days. She decides to give you a new horse after you set Cadillac free in the woods. I'm not sure if freeing him will be as politically rebellious as it sounds, but this is how it happens: Morgan reintroduces you to Cadillac; you tell her he is too much to handle; she asks you to give him another shot; he steps on a frog and kills it; you think about him stepping on you; he notices something he wants to eat and steps on your foot; you scream like you aren't supposed to; he stands on his back legs, and you let him eat whatever he's trying to get; he drinks from some sketchy-looking lake; you cry and debate going after him until you decide: *man, _____ Cadillac.* The nurse can't understand how a kid with hay fever and animal allergies ended up in horseback riding camp. She gives you purple pills while explaining the rest of your morning activity times will be spent in the medical cabin with her, Teddy Bear (the puppy), and the kid we will rename Flight because his current nickname is too problematic to be retold in the future.

Flight is easy to understand. He gets angry and needs medication to control his temper. You've never needed to take anything, but you've been hijacked by the same type of rage that drives him out of control. Flight flew off the handle a few times over the summer. He charged at you once, but you didn't move; this wasn't the fight he wanted or the one you were expecting. He calmed down, and you went back to learning about boon-doggle keychains and tetherball.

Other campers are impressed that you can back-flip off fences, chairs, but not into the pool. Ever since you almost drowned in second grade, you don't do water stunts. As, I'm sure you know by now, you're more worried about drowning than busting your head open. Second grade was pretty traumatic. Of course, there was that time you thought you were Knight Rider. There was also that time you saw a filmstrip about babies having a natural swimming instinct. Things went wrong when the instructor asked if you can swim, which is very different from do you know how to swim. You had the physical ability to swim but not the actual knowledge or practice. Watching all your friends dive in and swim reinforced your assumption about the swimming instinct. You knew those kids since kindergarten, and your school never offered any swim lessons until today. It never crossed your mind that different home lives taught different lessons, like swimming. You went for it. The instructor had to go in after you; your Speedo-style trunks started to fall off in the pool from the splashing around; the other kids were scared; it was bad. That day could be why you're here at summer camp swimming in basketball shorts with underwear underneath.

The kids in the locker room don't comment on your shorts, but they laugh at how you don't seem to have tan lines. Even the other Black kid aims jokes at you while reminding people his mother is white. You get on each other's nerves. Sometimes, when you walk into the cabin, you know they were talking about you because they freeze like you caught them with a mouth full of words they couldn't swallow. This isn't where the fight happens, but it's around the time you stopped drinking bug-juice and eating watermelon.

Dent explains the rules for a game called manhunt. It sounds like hide-and-seek, the official version, not any variants like hide-go-get-it, whooping-mamma, or hot peas and butter. Today's manhunt will be counselors versus campers. The idea is for you to hide in the woods and not be caught. If you are, you have to wait for another camper to free you from the holding area by tagging your hand without being captured. All of this seems like good wholesome fun until you realize you're a Black boy hiding in the woods in order to not be captured by a white hunter. When Growler spots you in the woods, he'll point and say he found one. He'll chase you while you hear the other kids call your name for freedom. You won't know what to do, so you'll keep running. The historical parallels will split you in half. Your body won't know if it should laugh or cry so it'll do both. Laugh because you'll think you're playing a game. Cry because you'll think you're playing a game. Growler won't be fast enough to catch you. You'll hide in the woods, laughing and crying as the night continues to fall. The counselors will get worried when they can't find you. They all will call your name again and again; they'll declare the game is over.

. . . and then the fight

Ain't no more making fun your skin
turning ashy between the pool and the sun.
Your mother done told you what to do
when common spaces shrink into whites-only
water fountains leaking formaldehyde. All summer
you done tried to ignore the fumes,
but ain't no asylum from the iron cast fixture
in the room. You hold amiability like a rusted toolbox
with no more wrenches. They see it
so they're extra nice, but that's them and not
the other Black kid. He looks at you
like he wants to fight you to prove he's not like you
or at least only half
as bad. He looks at you and laughs with them
like the sign above the fountain doesn't include him
on the more passable side of the code switch. You don't hear me
because you're in the moment
I look back on: the other kids cracking up,
the cabin falling to pieces;
his hands raising a statement he can't back up.
The toolbox is out the window. We still haven't met
and won't until your arm ratchets back;
and it does; and we do; and I become hesitation
asking your swing if it really want to throw this punch
knowing we been supposed to
set it on one of them white boys
but you didn't.

Campfire

Side A

A hundred years past
arguing about which activist deserves a mansion
we get an app that tallies those of us who die
in custody. It self-installs next to games
and widgets to be ignored. In the woods
where we still don't get service, forgotten name, drying
leaves piling—where we buried the grassroots
a swarm of hashtags trends away
if that is even still a thing. Children gather
like fireflies—their imaginations
a buzzing luminance—they share with each other
marshmallows and chocolate—one offers, who wants
a scary story. They lick their fingers. For howling spirits,
their mouths water. As the story goes,
they get police,
handcuffs,
and a jail cell,
and nobody flinches.
Not even when the plot thickens into a Black woman
hanging. Around the fire, the young lights flicker
unmoved in their apathy. They say, this ain't scary;
it happens all the time.

Side B

Police shot Tarika Wilson in her own home shot Breonna Taylor in her own home shot Atatiana Jefferson in her own home shot Aiyana Stanley-Jones in her own home shot Yvette Smith in her own home she was the one who called the police she was a seven-year-old she was playing video games she was in her bed her grandmother was there her nephew was there her children were there she didn't have a weapon she didn't go for the officer's gun she was set on fire by a flash grenade she wasn't the target the storyteller retorts *this ain't scary*
not even with all of the details
bleeding together?

Instrumentals

and fistfight

and gun pull

and smoke clear

and finger cross for

> *survival*
> > *when it is time to go*

> *back home*

Algebraic

Middle school hallway into high school together,
graduate varsity sports into bar fights together,
and people still think our relationship is less biological
because our Blackness appears as different
algebraic expressions people won't understand:
my grandfather, who will be his father, will be Black.
His mother, who will not be my grandmother,
will be white. Simple math will be this problem:
(X = Race + ISM + Color + ISM) ÷ (we won't look alike)

*What is the ratio of melanin to skin that will equal kin
when observed in a vacuum?*

Grandma Sylvia took one picture
with two of five known grandsons.
She does not know she is about to meet this math problem
for the first time. Since she landed
she has been in the kitchen cooking rice & peas
and mackerel rundown
and was asked never asked where she learned the recipe.
This would have been a question of who were her grandparents,
even more a question of how we could reach
back to the island that gave her to us
more a question of who are we
and why are we so good at keeping family secrets from family
even when the family secret is family?

What is the cubed root of a silent immigrant's inertia?

He nicknames himself Jamaica
in order to blacken his ambiguity.
I am too young to understand how
my Eastern Parkway flags are the same
attempt to express fractional parts
people reduce from us.

What is the surface area of an identity crisis
when (X + Y) = (first generation) ÷ American?

He isn't talking to me, and I'm not talking to him
and we aren't listening to mediation
because we think we have forever to heal
back to the family we were
like cancer didn't subtract his father
like that diagnosis won't return
a symmetrical death for him
before we reconcile.

What is the absolute value of a grudge that was never yours to levy
when time is a nonrenewable factor?

He cosigned my mixes out of basements
and the tangent was my first poem
on an open mic—we should have reconnected
before Leukemia made him a bed.
Now he is a ventilator
full of expiring discussions we can't have
because bar owners and promoters insist
my choice between a dancefloor and a last breath
is not equal to or greater than the cost of a flight
but my face is on their flier
next to the admission price and drink specials.

What is the centrifugal force of airfare to a funeral
on a body in distress?

Doctors imply a recovery, if we wait
for infections to clear. His mother plans
against their medical training and demands
chemotherapy. His immune system is rounded down
in the middle of the night. She calls my phone.
The signal drops. Dead air divides my sleep.

What are the biomechanics of circadian rhythms
divided at the rate of (self × blame) + (fault × pain)?

Instrumental

It's 2 PM. We get out of the white Toyota Paseo purchased from Yahoo Auction and tell Jason about a photo project we're working on for school. He agrees to let us shoot him and his two Rottweilers. We take allergy medicine and head to the park. Between shots, we mention the Technics SL-1200s we bought from an off-duty state trooper. He isn't sure what we're talking about; all he gets is we're still spinning, and maybe these turntables are better than the ones we ordered from the catalogue in the back of *The Source* magazine. We continue on about house parties, concerts, and talent shows. He mentions his security job at a new club. We invite him to hear how our mixes have grown since the Gemini XL BD10 days in our mother's basement. Back at our apartment, we record a practice session while he watches and listens. After we're done, he tells us to follow him downtown. We collect our promotional materials, get in our cars, and we're out.

It's 5 PM. Jason introduces us to a club owner. We hand over our mixtape and show the owner the press clips in our CVS photo album. He points at the photo album, says he doesn't need to see it, and tells us to put together an hour set because we're on tonight. We rush home and pack close to 200 vinyl records into plastic crates we found in a Rite Aid parking lot. This may seem like a lot of music for the amount of time we were given, but it isn't. The average rap, r & b, or reggae song is only about 3–4 minutes long, but there are a lot of factors to consider. What if you put on a good record at the wrong time and everybody walks off the dance floor? That song is wasted. You can't play it again. You're going to need an alternative. What if you need doubles of a twelve-inch single because you want to loop part of the beat or juggle between different versions of a song? What if you want to play different songs from the same album back-to-back? Unless it's one of the most amazing songs ever, it shouldn't play for more than half of its total duration. What if the previous DJ spins something you had planned for your set? Trust me, they will do this. Intentionally. What about set changings and transitions? You don't know what song the previous DJ will leave on the decks. What if they exit on some Joe Arroyo and you were ready to play DMX? You'll have to build into your set. This could take a couple of records. Remember, with all of these considerations, something always has to be coming out of those speakers.

It's 9:30. Jason and the other bouncers dress in black tank tops with fingerless gloves. When we walk in, he introduces us as his nephew. Nobody believes him. We walk to the DJ booth. He demands we play next. Instead of reminding him the booth is their domain, the other DJs comply and tell me to be ready. He gives us our handshake and walks away. We push our crates to the side and get our records ready. A woman in a snake-print catsuit asks the current DJ to play "Ryde or Die" by the Ruff Ryders. Her request is interesting because the room is responding well to "U Know What's Up" by Donell Jones. Breaking this mood doesn't seem like a good idea. We watch to see how the other DJ plays it. He does what so many DJs would do: plays "Get It On Tonight" by Montell Jordan and points our way. She aims her request at us. We respond, *sorry ma', we don't be taking requests.* She turns her head to the side in disbelief. Another DJ in the booth asks us to play her song. We agree but decide not to spin it right away. We need to figure out how to place it without a problem. Let's keep in mind this is a time in African America when anything DMX or The LOX will cause a fight. We actually keep their music in a section called The Snuff-Out Section. Songs filed here get people punched in the face when we play them in succession. Sometimes we run this whole set when a club owner or promoter makes us mad. We don't do this here, at least not today, because Jason is one of the bouncers and, as of right now, we haven't seen him tackle that cop at the front desk. He hasn't knocked that dude out in the alley yet either.

It's 10 PM. The woman in the catsuit is back. We promise her song is next, but it isn't. She believes us and dances away. The other DJ tells us not to play her song because they want her to come back. We pretend not to be nervous, but we are. We cue "The 900 Number" by The 45 King, let it play, and it works. We shout people out on the mic.

Our college friends start a dance cipher. The owner points and nods at us from the bar. We get brave and decide to risk some house music into this mix. The transition isn't as clean as we'd like, but people hear where we're trying to go and get excited. The party heats up. The cipher takes over the floor and proves "Hot Music" by Soho is absolutely the best house song of all time. Our boys are putting on a show with their moves, so we blend in "Joints & Jams (Billion Mix)." The vibe feels right until we see the woman in the snake-print catsuit. She is drunk and irritated. We don't know how long she's been there, but the other DJs are begging us to just play her song. We dig up the record along with "Head Banger" by EPMD, Redman, and K-Solo. Neither track feels appropriate for this set, but we show her the records. She walks away. Reluctantly, we drop the needle on the track and of course it does not work for the room. People look at the DJ booth and slowly walk off. The woman in the catsuit runs back accusing us of playing the wrong song. We point at the turntable, hold up the album cover, and shake our head. She recites lyrics to "Ruff Ryders' Anthem," a much more popular track from the exact same album. This is one of the problems with requests. Most people don't know song titles. They usually know hooks or a couple of lines and try to sing them to you over the blaring sound system. Back in the future, Shazam, smartphones, and YouTube make song requests easier to understand. Technology in 2024 will make requesters ask for even more obscure songs, and when you say no, they'll ask if they can plug their phones into your equipment. We'll worry about that when the time comes. Right now, we need people back on the dance floor. We reach for every AV8 and Fatman Scoop song that doesn't use an instrumental we've already played. "The Franklinz" and "Be Faithful" win the people back enough for us to transition into the *Bookshelf Riddim*. The other DJs seem unfamiliar with these songs. They look at us like we've just done a magic trick. We cover the label with our hand and hide the jackets so they can't see the title. Nobody is going to play this Riddim in this club except me. If people want to hear it again, then the other DJs have some homework to do, or the owner is going to have to bring us back. For our last song, we leave something easy for the next DJ to follow: "Real Love (Remix)." As

Mary J. Blige sings into Biggie's verse, we step to the side so the next DJ can transition into his set. He takes the record off the table, and hands it to us. As we walk down the stairs, Jason comes up, gives us our handshake, and, for the rest of the night, we walk around like we own the joint.

Hpnotiq Music

no tea / no cup / no spoon / no watch / the stir, a song / the swing / the beat / the cup, a booth / the cup, a dance / the cup, a floor, a floor / the watch, the dance / the spin / the speed / the bump / the shoulder / the push / the room / a record / a spin / a hand / a spin / deep, deep, the fall / the song / the words / the men / the drinks / the hearts, the beats / the women, a song / the music, a trance / the hands / the watch / the eyes / the watch / the hands / the spill / the dance / the spin / the speed / the spins / the shoulder / the bump / the floor, the ceiling / the air / the run / the air / the bottle / the flight / the air / the strike / the light / the strobe / the music / the fight / the strobe / the light / the strike / the mace / the fight / the spins / the cough / the end / the night.

Gun Groove

We are three deep at a party in a trap house. We know what it is because the stares are broken; and where the lawn should be, men slap-box for no reason more than the Saturday night: the sky, the lighting, the barbecue, the new sneakers, the girls watching, the no school tomorrow, all mixing with Wu-Tang Clan and Hennessy. Weed smoke and 40oz bottles sail and crash against the neighboring house. The kitchen illuminates the boundary between staying alive and being memorialized on a t-shirt. If you haven't come to cook up or cop, mind your door frames and stay in your place. From the brown plaid couch, feel the sound system repeat gunshots when new beats drop. Sing along to the bullets and chalk lines you know; and to the ones you don't, hum and mumble until you eventually memorize the crime scenes assembling in your imagination. Parents say this music will kill us. We don't hear them. We're in the dark, the music is loud, and the party just started. A girl dances you into a kiss against the wall. Her phone call was the invitation you followed here. Your hands slip into her back pockets, and she presses closer. Heat between you sweats down your backs and steams the windows. This drenching against each other pauses when a noise climbs over the speakers and pulls her away. She heads toward the kitchen. You offer to follow, but chivalry is a gesture she is too smart to let you die trying to perform. She promises herself back before the song ends. Anticipating her return makes genres become hours, artist names become minutes, and track titles become seconds. She left at R&B: SWV: I'm So into You. Now it's Reggae: Super Cat: Dolly My Baby, and she still isn't back.

Vinyl records continue to spin time forward. You're supposed to be where she left you, but curiosity carries you toward the kitchen. A different girl grabs your arm. The urgency she squeezes into your elbow bends you to her height. Her name is lost under a song you won't remember. She leads you outside. A man fights his way from the kitchen and is tackled before you leave. The tussle makes the needle jump, but the party doesn't stop because the whole house is bouncing. On the first landing, an unseen target swings on your back. It has been there the whole night.

It says the man collected back into the kitchen was coming for you. His birthday is on the other side of midnight. He looks bigger than the fine print on the invitation. Had you known this was his house you would have still been here because you're nineteen and willing to risk your life for a dark room and a girl you ultimately won't end up with. The party empties onto the street behind you. The girl explaining your rescue is without panic when she begs you to leave. Everybody's attention is broken when a black Pontiac burns rubber into the air. It rings the drive-by shooting alarm conditioned into all of us. Everybody runs. You think you're moving with the crowd. You feel yourself in flight, but your feet haven't lifted. You won't call this an out-of-body experience for another 20 years. By then, today will replay when fireworks blow you from your sleep. The car smokes past the house, stops at the end of the block, and backs up. The revving engine snarls to give you a head start, but your soul has already abandoned its body; if purgatory has a ghetto, it's down the street; it's in an empty field looking back at you. The transmission drops the car into drive, and the tires scream forward. On its second pass, you expect shots and brace yourself as the barrel stretches from the window. You pray for a gun jam, and maybe this is the song our parents warned us about, bullet cutting grooves in heavy rotation. We hope the shooter is also out of his body. We pray he sees us on this street and feels future guilt build a life sentence around him. The answered prayer is, you aren't hit. Your eyes open in time with your soul descending back into your body. The car takes the corner. You leave before the driver decides to take a second shot. On the way home, the friend you call cousin, and the cousin you call brother, suggest you didn't run because you thought you were hard. If they meant petrified, they're right.

Livestream

police cars

sirens

screams

cries   *tears*

emergency vehicles

The Position

The train came with a police officer

on his gun, his weight shifts
against the door, a flashback   the 1st time
a service weapon was in my face   the 2nd time
it made me get on the ground   the 3rd time
it put my hands in the air   the 4th time
it pushed me against a wall   the 5th time
it told me, it was doing its job   the 6th time
it kicked my feet apart   the 7th time
it grabbed my shirt collar   the 8th time

read the signs
it's illegal to move between cars

read the signs:
cop, gun, eye level

the safety told the trigger   the 9th time
we all look the same   the 10th time
under the right racism   the 11th time
the barrel cocked its head   the 12th time
and told me it missed me   the 13th time
and it was ready for the smoke   the 14th time
it dared me to swing   the 15th time
I thought about it   the 16th time
I almost did   the 17th time
there were no cameras   the 18th time
no phones   the 19th time
just covered badges   the 20th time

searching me for the broken laws it thought I was.

Exit Wounds

The white Custodian from the school where I teach
does the following:

- goes home
- kills his wife
- wounds his daughter while his son watches
- leads a high-speed car chase
- crashes into a gas station
- causes the gas pump to catch fire
- causes fire to catch his car

the security camera catches everything:

- The police officer out of his cruiser
- The police officer drawing his weapon
- The police officer walking toward the burning vehicle

See the bullet points; imagine them
loaded into a semi-automatic gavel.
Think about yourself
or myself
and the execution
of justice.

The White Custodian from the school that is
only minutes away from where Akai Gurley was murdered
continues:

- to open the door
- to wave his arm in a threatening manner
- to chase and tackle the officer

And you know what the officer does
not shoot him.

You know what, the officer does not shoot him.

You know what: the officer does not shoot him.

You know what the officer does: not shoot him.

You know what the officer does not: shoot him.

No matter how you cut it
. . . the officer does not shoot him; on the internet
he is not choked; in the middle of the street
no knee on his neck; he is taken alive
from where we would have been left
with exit wounds.

Deadass

They dead produce about 8 billion bullets a year
    dead have about 18,000 police departments
with about 700,000 sworn officers.   We dead know
there are about 28hrs before another one of us is dead
taken by the ammunition on patrol   and they dead what us
        to have faith in a system
where desk duty is punishment for Eric Garner strangled
    dead on camera they violate our civil rights
    and dead expect us not to fight or flight they   dead tell us
we should not be
resisting   George Floyd was dead on his face
  when they dead showed us
  they will dead dead us dead in the middle of the street
they shot Philando Castile dead in his own car
    dead in front of his girlfriend
    dead in front of their daughter
   he dead tried to comply   they dead shot him
   we dead saw the video   he dead died
    dead on livestream
  and they dead protested our protest with *all lives matter*
    dead protested our protest with *blue lives matter*
    dead protested our protest with *let the police do their job*
Isiah Brown dead got shot by the police he called
  and they dead want us to trust their training
when they dead mistake their tasers for their guns
    we dead be Daunte Wright
    we dead be Oscar Grant
   we dead be dead
  while they dead let their tongues go
    dead in their mouths

Shutter Speed

We're in the middle of the politically-charged-internet t-shirt craze.
Mine ties my contemporary self to my historical struggle
in a very simple way. It's black; it's cotton
and it says, *"We out."—Harriet Tubman.*
It's on my back. It's on my front. I'm wrapped in it
as I walk down the street. A white woman I do not know
puts her hand on my chest and says, *oh my god,*
you're not going to believe this, but I used to be a slave
in my past life. My past-self claps his hands
thinking about what he would do
if a white person put their hands on him. My future self
covers his face. He doesn't think people will believe
this actually happened. The self still in the t-shirt notices
her hand still on my chest, and worries
somebody might see this and not know
who the aggressor is. This white self-identified former slave woman
is now asking if she can take my picture.
When I refuse to let her shoot me,
when I refuse to let her get me shot,
she throws a tantrum. It lands under my skin. I feel
if I have to depend on public opinion to choose
between me and her tears, then an unwritten
police report is already preparing
to spin my dead body
away from what is actually happening. I wonder if she sees
the irony in her reincarnation claims.
She says, she remembers being a slave in her past life
but can't figure out why I won't let her capture me
in this one.

. . . and for our next trick, we attempt shopping

We approach the entrance and offer our bag
for inspection: no trapdoors, no false bottom;
security nods
without looking; we take this to mean they aren't
or don't want us to know they are, or we are
inside of our own head again
circling past false alarms. We scan record bins
and CD cases
and tapes on shelves
and secret shoppers
and count the holsters. They may not have
the album we're to buy, Digable Planets'
Blowout Comb. On the wall, concert fliers
and photocopies of shoplifters; downstairs
in the rap section, a cash register with a key
dangling trust to take a turn
no employees
no mirrors;
no, we aren't here to make anything disappear
not the music
not the money
not the life we left our house with
nothing up our sleeve
nothing in the small of our back.
The only sleight of hand is us shopping for nostalgia
and staying alive
while looking like a target from training videos
where muscle memory is taught
to jump the gun.

Fire Flame Fluency

An unanswered email wants my voice
on Floyd and Kaepernick and Black people
ever ready to take a knee. It asks, property damage
instead of body count—in the middle of protests
and my twice deleted response, flames take a police van
around the corner—its ignition, a kerosene reflex within
walking distance—parallel-parked between newspapers
and on t-shirts—it's burning steel
and burning rubber—through my sightlines
it follows me, I suspect, as it would
had it not met its match.
It would have never stalled its engine
or jammed its locks
or flattened its tires to protect me
from its driver's lead foot. It, too, was a weapon
and it, too, shall not prosper
and I, too, agree with the reverend, and, too, with the minister
who, too, were both taken and given back
as intersections where I, too, agree: violence is impractical
but how are we to negotiate when
the national dialect is riot and massacre:
see Colfax, Louisiana
see Wilmington, North Carolina
see Atlanta, Georgia
see Red Summer, all summer
see how we aren't dwelling in the past
the MOVE bombing happened in my lifetime;
see the helicopter
see the rowhouses
see how they want us fluent in fire
only when we are the ones burning.

Bonus track

a dark alley coughed up his body

... and then they found Rasta Mike

Neighborhood: He owed too much money.

Streets: You can't sell weed and have a crack problem.

Corner: That's not drug dealing.

Right Hand: He had a gun, but he sold it.

Police:

Wife: Mi neva tell dem nuttin
wen dem run up inna mi yaad and look fi him.
Dem cudda kill mi and mi pickney
and mi neva tell dem nuttin.

Police:

News: Children discover dead body.

Kids: We was outside playing.

Girlfriend: We was in the house smoking.

Police:

Autopsy: Victim suffered numerous gunshots.

Neighborhood: In the face.

Kids: In the alley.

Police:

We still haven't solved what happened to Little Tasha.

Acknowledgments

Before thanking institutions involved in making this book possible, I have to acknowledge family members, biological and chosen, who supported me and allowed parts of their personal lives to be between these pages.

Thank you to my mother. Without you, no version of me exists. I love you and am immensely grateful for you. Before I was old enough to write, you nurtured my voice by letting me tell you stories until your exhausted body fell asleep after holding down multiple jobs and graduate school responsibilities. From spinning on the kitchen floor, deejaying in the basement, and writing poems in notebooks, you were there at every stage of my creative journey. When I saw you reading the advanced copy of this book, I was worried about what you would think. Thank you for permitting me to share our stories with the world. I hope you know nothing makes me prouder than being able to say I'm Debbie's son.

Courtenay, you're the little sister I prayed to have. Thank you for your research, recordkeeping abilities, and many subscriptions that allowed me to access national archives worldwide. Your knowledge of our family and Black history helped fill segments of this book that would have fallen apart without you.

Mayor, the honesty and vulnerability you shared throughout my life is uncharacteristic for men in our family. While my father wasn't around how he should have been, you treated me less like a nephew and more like a son. There was a difficult time in my life when you told me to drop everything I was carrying physically and emotionally and insisted I follow my love for poetry and music; the stories from days in your room and in your Isuzu Trooper became poems and reflections that continue to help me understand us and how I got here. Thank you for being the uncle I needed and the dad I never had.

RIP, Uncle Danny. Your drive to pursue art inspired me to write poems contained in this collection. You gave me the city and put me on my first stage, and I have yet to diverge from your example.

RIP, Uncle Jason. You took me to my first open mic. You also got me my first DJ residency at a nightclub. I've played around the world and published books since then. We dreamed of this. I'm sorry you're not here physically to celebrate it with me.

RIP, Nana. Thank you for preserving all the pictures and stories. You left just enough clues for me to travel the world and reassemble our family when our citizenship status became safe enough to do so. I've never missed anybody as much as I miss you.

RIP, Skip. Writing about you, looking at your pictures, and reading your letters have been an investigation of masculinity in our family for generations. Taking time to see you beyond the painful mythology I inherited gave me helpful context to understand you, my uncles, the men around me, and myself in a more focused and processable light.

RIP, Aunt Betty. Thank you for gradually letting me into the memories you keep buried. I'm still finding the people we discovered together.

Neil, thank you for reminding me to tell these family stories respectfully and sensitively.

Thank you to my all my international family in Cuba, Jamaica, Bermuda, Brazil, and Panama. *Gracias*, Karina, David, y Gisela por *permitir que nuestra familia se reconecte.*

While thanking my family, I can never forget Mahogany L. Browne. You've been in my corner since we met and never let anybody or any organization look past me or my work. You encouraged me to quit my day job and follow writing as a career path; I know this experience is not unique to me. As Adam Falkner said in your documentary, "Mahogany L. Browne has created more space for young writers to grow into themselves than anybody working in American Letters, and if you take Mahogany L. Browne out of that equation, there are thousands of writers who flat-out don't exist." I wholeheartedly agree with this statement while being aware of how your name habitually gets excluded from acknowledgment; the erasure you frequently experience speaks to how our society accepts, and in many cases insists upon, the labor of Black women while disregarding their presence and personhood. I see, recognize, appreciate, and love you. Thank you for supporting me and this project from concept to completion. Without you, *Skip Tracer* would have stalled and decayed in the back of my mind.

Amare Symoñe, thank you for your insight on digital marketing and promotions; our conversations about rollout demonstrated your well-informed understanding of digital space, the author, and the intentionality behind *Skip Tracer*. As I thank you with love and appreciation, I hope you continue to give sound to the songs in your heart. I've watched you sing and explore music since you were three. No matter what you do, whether you choose composing music or promotional copy, continue to sing for that little girl in Bed-Stuy.

Charlotte Sheedy, you sifted through this project's original confusion and found buried parts that need more visibility. Your support, patience, advice, and willingness to stand by this work is why it ended up in the hands of its publisher. Instead of rejecting the *Skip Tracer* manuscript and explaining why it would never be successful, you put me in conversations with editors and readers willing to understand, interpret, and guide it through developmental stages. Thank you for taking a chance on me and believing in *Skip Tracer*.

Ally Sheedy and Miranda Barry, your keen eyes, comprehension, and understanding of the work sparked new ideas and concepts that expanded it unexpectedly. There were moments when I felt like I was spinning in circles. Our conversations helped me regain traction and move forward.

Erika Stevens, thank you for joining the team and translating many confusing ideas between the publisher and me. I enjoyed our meetings, conversations, and the ideas you shared.

Liveright Publishing, thank you for accepting an author who exists so far from your tradition. Your willingness to edit and publish *Skip Tracer* without intruding on its integrity allowed space for my creativity to challenge what I thought was possible on the page. The team was patient with my process and did their best to accommodate its quirks.

Christian Hawkey, thank you for remaining engaged in *Skip Tracer*'s construction through its many iterations; there were years of name changes and structural reconfigurations, and you were always willing to meet, hear me out, and offer suggestions that strengthened my ideas. Before our meetings on Fulton Avenue, I never considered writing or publishing long-form work. The graduate program you built allowed me and this project to grow beyond my conceptual limitations.

Tongo Eisen-Martin, your mission of bringing poetry to the people honors Black political and literary traditions in an immediately necessary way. Seeing you sharing my poem "City Clutter" from a previous collection inspired this book's "Clearing Clutter" piece. Showing me how my words impacted those young men behind the wall reinforced my desire to write for and to our unseen and forgotten community members.

Lynne Procope, you asked questions about *Skip Tracer* I never thought about or didn't know how to answer. Your mastery of language, cultural intelligence, honesty, and desire to foster excellence is why you continue to be among the few readers I trust with my work before it goes into the world.

Roger Bonair-Agard, you're the first poet I saw perform with a Trinidadian accent. My West Indian identity rarely appeared in my writing before that Harlem night. Now, there is a whole book named after my Jamaican grandfather. When many people dismissed my work without offering guidance, you sat with me in random locations to edit ideas that would become full-length poems in the collection; recalling those times reminds me of how much we, Black men, need each other and spaces for private dialogue and exchange. It is in those settings where we can talk, get things right, get things wrong, learn, heal, and grow the versions of ourselves that we and our communities need. Sometimes, those moments are at Popeye's in East New York, Brooklyn.

Thank you to the people who agreed to blurb this book. All of you are writers I deeply respect, and I feel honored that you were willing to support the project.

Nicole Sealey, whenever I read one of your poems, I find a new and exciting lesson for myself and my students. Your writing is clever and elegant in a way that makes it appreciated in every setting where I've shared it. I feel honored that such a writer agreed to blurb my book.

Terrance Hayes, I've heard of you through legend and folklore for years. I'm glad we got to know each other in the real world. You're a literal genius. Your suggestion to develop a poetic scaffolding helped me implement the mixtape and sound system structure. Thank you for reading the many versions of this book. Your input was concise, thoughtful, and greatly appreciated. In a world where writers get lost in preserving their own success, your generosity and consideration are unbelievable gifts.

Jason Reynolds, I'm unsure if people always see how invested you are in the success of underrepresented writers. Your ability to produce impactful work while pulling other writers through the door deserves recognition. The notes you offered after reading *Skip Tracer* at the Rhode Island Writers Colony inspired a series of new projects. Thank you. Future practitioners looking to navigate the literary world while maintaining authenticity will study you, the movements you've forged, and your approach to communal prosperity.

Mitchell S. Jackson, your presence in the literary landscape reminds me that my life is a shared experience and doesn't need to be polished or digestible at all times. We've seen each other at events a couple of times; during each interaction, you did or said something that indicated your willingness to keep it real at all times. Reading your words on the back of this book feels like hearing a familiar voice from a parallel community where only a few of us dodged the traps and survived the pitfalls.

Adam Falkner and Whitney Greenaway, you were the first readers to comment on *Skip Tracer* outside of my grad school environment. Thank you. As you both know, I love and respect you and value your command of language on the page and stage. I knew your observations would enhance the work and make it what it is today.

Jon Sands, there was a point when I was deleting and reformatting this book into an unrecognizable state. You saved me from what could have been a very destructive editing spiral. Your feedback assured me *Skip Tracer* was performing the tasks programmed into its construction.

Rico Frederick, we've collaborated in almost every art form I can draw to mind: graphic art, video production, deejaying, and poetry. Your eye for layout and technical skills helped me visualize this book's typographical designs. Thank you for tirelessly looking at drafts and advising their execution. Remember, *only a hard dozen!*

Christina Olivares, "Trademarks" would not have been possible without your translation in Cuba. Thank you for spending your vacation helping me reconnect with my family.

Thank you, Steve Goldbloom, *Brief but Spectacular*, PBS, and *Verses and Flow*, for airing early versions of work in this collection.

Thank you, David and Alex, in Bristol, for treating me like family while I was doing research in the UK.

Thank you, Dasha Kelly, for the documentaries that got me interested in family research.

Thank you, Carlos Andrés Gómez, for hours discussing this project with me over a Waffle House omelet in Atlanta.

Southern Fulton Institute, you gave me a month to think and write in an environment that asked me to do nothing more than focus on my art. *Skip Tracer* is the project I worked on while living in your community.

Thank you to all the libraries and research centers: National Archives (Washington DC), National Archives (NYC), National Archives in Kew Garden(England), and National Archives (Jamaica).

Supa Dupa Fresh curators and audience, thank you for being a community where I could experiment with almost all these pieces during the creative process.

Thank you, Academy of American Poets and *No, Dear* magazine, for publishing early versions of work printed in this collection.

Skip Tracer was only possible with the support of individuals and organizations who saw its potential over the years. I appreciate everybody who answered questions, took me on tours, translated languages, shared stories, and responded to random direct messages and emails. If I forgot your name, group, or institution in this section, please accept my apologies and know I value you, and your contributions were significant. Thank you for your love and encouragement.